May you increasingly come to
o relish storytelling
o champion public speaking
o aspire to greatness in oratory

With Best Wishes

Roslin

Necessary Bridges

Public Speaking & Storytelling for Project Managers & Engineers

Rashid N. Kapadia

ISBN: 9780990646105

Library of Congress Control Number: 2014915683

Cover designed by The Art of Books
markgelotte.com

First Edition

Printed and bound in the United States

With infinite gratitude I dedicate this work to ...
My parents, for their limitless love and their
sterling examples. And for invaluable memories
of contentment, erudition and equanimity.

My wife and son, for their limitless love and
their selfless support. And for making us the blessed
family we are.

I would also like to dedicate my work to ...
All engineers and project managers, past, present and
future. Alas, too often, "the world little knows ... nor
long remembers ..." the greatness of our professions.

All who bring passion and purpose to public
speaking, storytelling and oratory.

All who set audacious goals, long to build necessary
bridges and make the world a better place.

Contents

Preface

"It always seems impossible until it is done."
— Nelson Mandela

I remember being truly mesmerized, watching a scene from the movie *Invictus*. This is the scene in which the president of South Africa summons the captain of its national rugby team to his presidential office, and plants the seed of an idea: "Win the Rugby World Cup; our broken nation needs this of you. Together, we must all become 'One Team, One Nation.'"

This movie portrays a portion of the multifaceted book called *Playing the Enemy* by John Carlin. It is one of the best sports books I've read, covering one of the greatest sports stories of all time; but it is much more. It is an inspirational self-help book. It is a book about a political genius who faced multiple impossibly difficult challenges, and who responded with, "It always seems impossible until it is done." It is a book about an epic injustice and an epic reconciliation. It is a book about a leader, who perhaps more than anyone else on this planet, mastered the art of making friends and influencing people. It is a book about a superb public speaker. It is a book, which describes the most unlikely exercise in political seduction ever undertaken. And it is a book, which led to a superb scene in a marvelous movie.

President Nelson Mandela (NM): Tell me, Francois, ... what is your philosophy of leadership? How do you inspire your team to do their best?

Captain of the Springboks Rugby team, Francois Pienaar (FP): By example ... I've always thought to lead by example, Sir.

NM: Well that is right ... that is exactly right. But how to get them to be better than they think they can be? That is very difficult, I find. Inspiration, perhaps. How do we inspire ourselves to greatness, when nothing less will do? How do we inspire everyone around us? I sometimes think it is by **using the work of others.**

On Robben Island, when things got very bad ... I found inspiration in a poem.

FP: A poem?

NM: A Victorian poem ... just words ... but they helped me to stand when all I wanted to do was to lie down.

But you didn't come all this way to hear an old man talk about things that make no sense.

FP: No, no, please Mr. President ... it makes complete sense to me. On the day of the big match, say a test, in the bus, on the way to the stadium, nobody talks.

NM: Ah yes, they are all preparing.

FP: Right. But when I think we are ready, I have the bus driver put on a song, something I've chosen, one we all know ... and we listen to the words together ... and it helps.

NM: I remember when I was invited to the 1992 Olympics in Barcelona. Everybody in the stadium greeted me with a song. At the time the future ... our future, seemed very bleak. But to hear that song in the voices of people from all over our planet made me proud to be South African. It inspired me to come home and do better. It allowed me to expect more of myself.

FP: May I ask, what was the song, Sir?

NM: Well ... it was Nkosi Sikelel' iAfrika ... a very inspiring song.

We need inspiration, Francois, ... because in order to build our nation, we must all exceed our own expectations.

https://www.youtube.com/watch?v=TQhns5AwAkA

I wondered why this scene moved me so deeply. I thought long and hard about it. Engineers all too frequently cannot leave great feelings, or well enough alone. They try to "figure it out." You already know this. I wasn't really satisfied with anything I initially came up with. That changed after I was exposed to the worlds of public speaking and storytelling.

After spending a few years trying to improve my public speaking and storytelling skills, I got a much better appreciation and understanding of why I was so mesmerized by the powerful *Invictus* scene. It is the same power that public speakers and storytellers everywhere attempt to harness.

I know I want to exceed my own expectations on a regular basis. Who doesn't? But to hear and see it dramatized this way was a game changer.

Vikas Jhingran has written a book called *Emote: Using Emotions to Make Your Message Memorable.* In his approach (with his uniquely analytical articulation of the role of emotions in speech craft), he recommends that we start writing a speech after having made a clear decision of the "final emotion" we want to leave the audience with.

Well, the emotions that I was left with at the end of this scene would be a fabulous way to feel at the end of any speech or presentation—regardless of whether I was in the audience or speaking to an audience.

I have drawn much inspiration from the movie Invictus, and especially from using **the work of others.**

In *Necessary Bridges*, I have used **the work of others** extensively. I acknowledge with much gratitude all that is available to us on the road to exceeding our own expectations. I have meticulously credited sources. Whenever I have cited the work (or the words) of others, I have italicized them. In the unlikely event I have inadvertently omitted to cite a source, I apologize in advance. The oversight error is entirely my own.

To the reader, if I have cited sources in a way that seems excessive, and occasionally disrupts the smooth flow of reading, or requires you to read too much italicized font, I ask your indulgence. It is an essential compromise: I ask your understanding.

Over many years as a project manager and engineer, it became clearer and clearer to me project managers and engineers were inadvertently compromising their professional and career advancement by not being "good enough" in public speaking and storytelling.

I committed to write this book because I inadvertently stumbled into a hole. I became aware of a gap, a mismatch; one that I could no longer ignore.

Briefly, these conclusions dawned on me: (1) there is a mismatch between what project managers know they need to excel at: and with what they commit to excelling at: and (2) there is a mismatch between what engineers think they need to know and learn: and with what they really need to know and learn. Put differently, this topic found me and in an inexplicable way commanded me to act! "Write a book, Rashid. Evangelize public speaking and storytelling to project managers and engineers. In time they will thank you for this contribution to our professions." A bonus benefit: Writing a book on a subject helps the author become an expert on that subject.

The primary purpose of this book is to get project managers and engineers to commit to acquiring expertise in public speaking and storytelling. The secondary purpose is to provide (just) enough content (accompanied by exercises, examples and directions to other resources—i.e. the work of others) to keep the commitment strong and sustained over years. There is plenty of marvelous content out there.

This book is NOT about technical presentations or presentations specific to the professions of engineering and project management. The content of this book is generic and exposes the reader to the basics of public speaking and storytelling.

This analogy may help explain my thinking. In the 1970s there was a revolution in which personal computers began entering our lives in a major way. Two dominant companies driving this revolution were Microsoft and Apple. Microsoft focused on providing really useful and ubiquitous products, but they were (in my opinion) not too concerned, perhaps even indifferent, to the design and the beauty of the products. Apple, on the other hand (in my opinion), was deeply concerned about the design and beauty of its products, perhaps obsessively so.

I see the Microsoft approach as one to which possibly engineers and project managers (at least of my age and background) default. Certainly that was my approach. I mean, "Who cares what it looks like as long as it works well?" It was only after the stunning success of products like the iMac, the iPod, the iPhone, the iPad, the MacBook Air etc., that the advantage of great design dawned on many of us.

I have come to believe that deciding to lavish deliberate attention and care on public speaking and storytelling can make the same difference to our professions that Apple's "design is very important" approach made to the computer (and computer-based consumer devices) industry.

This book has been conceived and created more as a product to be used in combination with other resources, than as a stand-alone book. It has been developed as a guide book providing course work. It has been conceived as an incubator of and companion to a self-development project, of minimum two years duration. It has been conceived with the intention that the reader will return to it multiple times over the duration of the self-development project, and read it along with other recommended books simultaneously. This is also called syntopical reading.

Indeed, here is a sample recommendation. I recommend that you procure a book called *How to Read a Book: The Classic Guide to Intelligent Reading* by Mortimer J. Adler and Charles Van Doren, and read that book in parallel with *Necessary Bridges*. You will extract much more value out of *Necessary Bridges* if you follow this approach.

It is my hope (dare I say vision), that someday in the not too distant future, project managers and engineers will routinely be thought of not only as smart and educated individuals, but as excellent public speakers and storytellers too; the way Apple products are thought of as marvels of engineering and are beautifully designed, too. Why? Because these are essential skills to move any human endeavor along. Public speaking and storytelling are essential skills to (using a line from Apple's Think Different ad) *"to push the human race forward."* Public speaking and storytelling skills are lubricating oils that keep the machinery of engineering, project management and relationship management running super-smoothly. And engineers and project managers have moved — indeed, pushed — the world forward as much as or more than any other profession.

It is my hope that engineers and project managers increasingly communicate in a way that leaves everyone around them experiencing the same final emotion I felt at the end of the *Invictus* movie scene; inspired and committed to exceeding their own expectations.

It always seems impossible until it is done!

Chapter 1

Who Am I?

*"Knowing others is intelligence; knowing yourself
is true wisdom. Mastering others is strength;
mastering yourself is true power."*
— *Lao-Tzu*

Hello, My name is Rashid N. Kapadia. I have been an engineer for more than 35 years and a project manager for almost 20 years. I consider engineering and project management to be two of the world's great professions. In the years and decades to come, I hope these professions will attract more and more of the best of the best.

One of my life's missions is to evangelize public speaking and storytelling to project managers and engineers. Presently, in my judgment, public speaking and storytelling are not adequately acknowledged or utilized by either profession. I would like this to change. This is the raison d'être for *Necessary Bridges*.

A well-known public speaker Mark Brown has said, "Your life tells a story and there's someone out there that needs to hear it."

I now ask you to commence an EXERCISE. Let's call it EXERCISE #1. Write down your life story in no less than 5,000 words. Make it as detailed as you can. It is OK to take months, even a year to complete it. Please make it deliberately long.

Why deliberately long? It is a set-up for an essential public speaking skill—that of speaking with clarity and brevity. My deliberately long story appears later in this chapter. You are welcome to use it as an example or as a template. Later in this book, I will set myself the challenge of converting my deliberatively long narrative, my life story, into a four-to- six-minute speech, frequently called an Icebreaker. I will invite you to create your icebreaker speech in parallel with mine.

Allowing for my public speaking rate of 100-125 words per minute, I will have to capture the essence of my deliberately long life story, using no less than 400 words and no more than 750 words. A delightful challenge! I love it!

Comparing the written version of my story to my Icebreaker speech will allow us to contrast two very different writing skills. Writing for the eye (memos, messages, letters, chapters, blogs and essays) is what all of us project managers and engineers do routinely and effortlessly. We are probably pretty good at it. Writing for the ear (speeches) is very different. We project managers and engineers practice this less frequently, too infrequently, I will argue. We probably pay a professional advancement price for this omission. I reiterate, these are very different skills—and both are critical for a rounded and upwardly mobile professional-life-voyage.

This is my *first wish* for you. "May you always have a wonderfully rounded and upwardly-mobile professional life!"

If you opt to do EXERCISE #1, to writing down your life story, please commit to taking it very seriously. It may well be one of the most important exercises you ever undertake—for it leads to self-knowledge, to knowing yourself, to mastering yourself, to true wisdom and to true power. This exercise, writing down your imperfect life story, imperfectly, leads to emotional intelligence. This exercise gives you permission to be vulnerable and flawed. We are all flawed. Accept it, get used to it and start writing. This exercise will require some courage. There are many very good reasons to complete this exercise. So just start.

After you start, a struggle will follow. You will want to stop. You will want to quit. It is simply going to happen. Your mind will invent clever—perhaps brilliant—stories and excuses, telling you why you should stop, or why you should procrastinate; why it is OK to do it later. Suck it up, ignore it, argue back, do whatever works ... but continue writing down your life story, and commit to completing it. Set a deadline; make a promise to someone who cares about you and will fearlessly (at your insistence) hold you accountable if and when you falter.

Quotations like this helped me. I hope they help you too. *"Know your enemy, and know yourself, and in a hundred battles you will never be in peril."* — Sun Tzu, 500 BC. Here's another quotation to keep you going: *"Know yourself. Don't accept your dog's admiration as conclusive evidence that you are wonderful."* — Ann Landers

If you opt not to do EXERCISE #1—ever, it will allow for a safe prediction: "You will not become a truly compelling speaker—ever." A million apologies for this candor; I wish I had better news for you; I don't.

More than anything else in the world, your audiences want to know you, or to identify with you, or to learn from you, or to root for you (not always—but the exception proves the rule), or to connect with you, or to remember you, or to have a good time when you are speaking. I reiterate; your audiences are looking for this from you; they want to be informed, to be entertained, to be motivated or to be inspired. Do not do a great disservice to your audience, even disrespect your audience, by not being authentic ... by not knowing yourself. You do not have the right to!

If you prefer to jump right into the learning of public speaking and storytelling, I request you proceed directly to chapter 2 from here. Please return to this point, my story, just before chapter 14. If you prefer to start off by learning a little bit more about me, which requires reading a deliberately long narrative, here it is.

My Story

My early years and education

My twin brother and yours truly were born in India in the late 1950s. Having a twin is a blessing like no other. I am a fortunate man.

I was raised in a home full of contentment, abundant energy and love, alongside an unyielding expectation of high standards. My parents were comfortably off; my father had his own business. My parents were leading and rock-solid members of their society—respected, admired and liked by the larger community. Mum and Dad were excellent role models who lived disciplined lives. Besides my twin brother, I have two wonderful sisters. I am a lucky guy.

My parents devoted a lot of their time and energy to public service. For my father, this was mostly through Rotary International. Dad held many officer positions, all on a voluntary service leadership basis. He travelled widely and frequently to carry out his Rotary duties. His good heart and lifelong commitment to uplift and provide for those less fortunate than us will always be a North Star that guides me. Additionally Dad was a splendid organizer (it wasn't called project management back then—but that is exactly what it was) and a superb persuader. He was a driving force behind many of the successful charitable works and projects undertaken during his Rotary years. His awesome public speaking prowess was a force multiplier.

It has often been said that you are an authentic leader only if you can lead a group of volunteers. In voluntary leadership, "responsibility without authority" is the only game in town. In this game, barking out orders gets nothing accomplished: Nothing at all. Project managers know this better than most.

Providential are those who excel in authentic leadership. I know my Dad did.

My father passed away almost seven years ago, and that resulted in a profound change somewhere deep inside of me. I knew then, and I know now, that he lives forever, inside of me. If I have ever spoken well, or indeed done anything well in my life, it is because of his many bequeaths to me. He lives in me. I am an ambassador for all he stood for.

Mum brilliantly and boldly supported Dad in all he did, provided leadership whenever called on, held home and hearts together, and set a lifelong gold standard for self-discipline. In the recent past, I spent about a month in my hometown in India with her. Every morning she would switch on my room lights at 4:30 and we would be out for our morning walk at 5. The pace was brisk, around 11 minutes/ km. Mum is in her 80s and I am in my mid-50s. I loved it!

As a young boy, when Dad was a Rotary district governor, I used to travel to nearby towns with him, and listen to him speak to his clubs. I was mesmerized listening to him and felt so proud to be his son. Even as a young child I felt motivated to join in and contribute. When I saw the respect others accorded him, deep inside, I felt wonderful. Being an excellent speaker and communicator gave Dad many distinguishing advantages. Truly, I am a fortunate man to have had this exposure through childhood and youth.

I went to three different schools, in three different states in India. The final six years of primary schooling were in an excellent, even elite, boarding school. Here I learned responsibility, resilience, and self-reliance. I developed the ability, at a very young age, to have good relationships with others from very diverse backgrounds. Social class, family wealth and religion counted for naught in boarding school:

naught, nothing, zero! We clustered into groups based primarily on personality and character, and secondarily around interests. School's goal was to provide a well-rounded education, which included lots of sports, some debating, some arts, some music, and many other extra-curricular activities. I was truly fortunate to have passed though the portals of this hallowed century-old institution.

After high school I began an undergraduate science degree, but dropped out to join a marine engineering apprenticeship program. It was here in the shipyard that my love of engineering was born and continuously kindled.

Through school and college, I was (at best) an average student who studied moderately. I do not remember being truly fired up by any of the subjects. That changed after I started my apprenticeship. Suddenly physics and mathematics came alive in the shipyard. They were living and breathing all around me. For the first time ever, I appreciated all the theory that I had rote-memorized. Its practical application was thrilling. It felt really good to know the physics and mathematics that designed the equipment I was working on. I began self-studying general marine engineering knowledge and marine diesel engine knowledge, far beyond any immediate academic requirements.

In our shipyard, over four years, we were rotated through many departments and workshops, including the diesel workshop, the fitting workshop, the machine shop, the platers and millwright workshop, the piping workshop, the electrical workshop, the welding workshop, and the new construction workshop. Sometimes we were assigned to "outside" teams, to repair or overhaul marine equipment on board ships in the commercial docks or in the naval docks. Other times we were assigned to dry docks. We spent a few months in the drafting offices learning the basics of engineering drawing. It was a beautifully rounded program—with one major weakness. As far as learning went, we were basically on our own. Completely and totally on our own.

Each morning the yard or shop foreman would assign us to work with some of his men, working on various repair and overhaul projects, usually valves, pumps, compressors, engines, rudders, propellers, etc. To the foremen and workers, we apprentices were basically cheap labor. In order to learn, we had to befriend the workers in the shop and tap into their goodwill and knowledge. Had I not been confident or lacked the ability to speak well and connect, my learning would have been cripplingly compromised.

This environment required significant initiative from us apprentices. We formed loose networks of friends and would keep each other abreast of all the interesting works going on in the yard. In time we formed a small group and started meeting regularly to discuss, in depth, the ongoing jobs and equipment we were exposed to. We were slowly but surely becoming engineers. Many of these meetings were at my flat (apartment) in Bombay, now renamed Mumbai. We would get together to practice engineering drawing, too. Back then we were given six hours to complete drawing a component. Occasionally an officer from the yard would join our small group, eager learners, and take us to another level with his knowledge and stories of past projects and challenges. It was exhilarating. There are few joys greater than seeking and acquiring new knowledge—surrounded by friends and peers.

We also spent some time in the local marine-engineering college, in a classroom environment, learning mechanics, heat and heat engines, drawing, etc. This time around, I appreciated and loved classes, and participated at a level way beyond my average efforts in school and college. I was driven to learn, and made sure that I understood why each part was included in any machine, its design, and its purpose.

While the yard work was interesting and frequently fascinating, mostly I loved the large two-stoke marine diesel engines; true engineering marvels!

My career

On completing the four-year marine engineering apprenticeship program, and on completing the first of many certificate of competency exams, I started sailing on merchant marine ships. The work was hard, the engine room temperatures were mostly between 45 and 55 degrees Centigrade (110–130 degrees Fahrenheit), and we were "watch-keeping" around the clock. My first ship *Jag Ratna* hardly sailed; she was mostly stuck at anchorage. As the junior-most engineer officer, I ended up keeping night watch —12 hours each night, 6 p.m. to 6 a.m.—for 20-30 days every month for 10 straight months. Reality of a marine engineer's life at sea was beginning to set in.

I continued sailing over a period of 12 years, took more certificate of competency exams and specialty courses, and made it to the top rank, chief engineer. I sailed with more nationalities, personalities, and characters than I can hope to remember. I had Indian, Hong Kong, British, Singaporean, and Scandinavian shore-based bosses. I sailed on general cargo vessels, crude oil tankers, product tankers, chemical tankers, ore-bulk-oil carriers, container ships, and refrigerated cargo vessels. Some vessels were old; junk really, while some were new and magnificent. I even got to take a brand new 150,000 tonner out from the yard. I sailed with some awesome engineers and leaders, and I endured my fair share of CBT (cynical, bitter, and twisted) shipmates.

My many years at sea taught me a few enduring lessons.

Back then there was minimum communication between shore and ship, and what little there was, was expensive. Effectively, the engineering teams were alone; on their own; no technical help from the outside world. With the exception of a crippling breakdown, if there was a problem, we had to find a fix on our own. Period. A ship may be thought of as a floating and moving island, and it was up to us, marine engineers, to do the needful to support life and make the next port.

I learned:

1. There is always a way. There is always a way.

2. Getting along nicely with all, including strangers and strange cultures, is the best option. Conflict, squabbling, moaning, and bitching may be unavoidable, but these are simultaneously suboptimal. Don't like other people? Don't like other characters? Don't like other cultures? Look for common interests, and unyieldingly, direct attention to these common interests. I learned this lesson well. In the final analysis, we are not that different from each other!

3. Constant learning is the only way forward.

During my sailing years, my sweetheart and I got married. We have one child, a precious son, and our God-given nonpareil gift. My wife and son sailed with me a lot. I used to joke with some of the young cadets at sea that my son has more "sailing time" than they did.

My wife and I have frequently been told that we are a blessed couple: Yes we are! Our son is the greatest, greatest treasure of our lives; all else is a very, very distant second. This fortunate man is part of a super-blessed family.

Over my sailing years, I decided:

1. There is more to life than this. I need a plan to move on.

2. I want to be there for my son as he is growing up. A great salary is something I can live without. Sure, I would prefer it; but I will survive. These growing up years of my son will never come back.

3. I will leave this life after making it to chief engineer. I will do no more than three voyages as a chief engineer. Then it's over.

Our family moved to the US in the mid-1990s, a risky move. I came here as a graduate student. I was in my mid-30s. We were well aware that we were effectively giving up a life of assured comfort, a very good and solid income, and rock solid stability. The future was an unknown—uncharted waters. I spent an intense initial period upgrading my education and qualifications. I took a post-graduate marine management degree, and other professional maritime business certification courses: agency, chartering, admiralty, maritime economics, and others

Once, during post-graduate work, I had to give our class a presentation. During this presentation, to my utter shock, I found myself physically shaking. I had walked up and started speaking with my customary high confidence, and then, out of nowhere, the shakes came on. This was stunningly unexpected: I was furious at myself! I naturally presumed that my audience saw and sensed my nervousness—all of it. It never even occurred to me to seek feedback. Looking back now, I seriously doubt that anyone even noticed my sudden and wholly unexpected onslaught of nervous shakes. And today, I never "not seek feedback" after a speech or presentation.

You must know that I had routinely participated in debates throughout my school and college days—so this public speaking thing was certainly not new territory for me.

In school and college, debates included many forms of public speaking. Declamation was famous speeches, which we had to memorize and deliver—like: *"Friends, Romans, countrymen, lend me your ears ..."* or like: *"Long years ago we made a tryst with destiny ... ."* We had elocution—reciting poetry. "Inchcape Rock," "Casabianca," and "The Charge of the Light Brigade" are indelible school-day memories. We had debates where two teams were given a topic, and one debated for, and another against. We had extemporaneous where we were given a topic and a few minutes to prepare a three-minute speech. Finally, we had the usual prepared speech where we had to write and deliver our own original content. So that was a lot of practice, over many years. I recall with amazement the number of speeches and poems I had completely memorized. I am fortunate to have had these splendid opportunities so early in life.

I participated regularly in all formats of debates, and—please pardon my disgraceful lack of modesty here—I was pretty good.

So you can imagine my consternation at feeling like a postgraduate-student rookie and getting nervous shakes in front of a known audience. Yes, it had been more than 15 years since I had last spoken publicly—but still—me ... getting nervous? No, no, no, no, no! ... Simply unacceptable! It was a truly sobering and humbling experience. Truth be told, I actually felt humiliated.

Thankfully, I cleared all my professional and advanced exams at the first attempt. This is more of an achievement than it may sound like. I put this down to the early influence and expectations of my parents, the infinite support of my wife, and my love of learning. Or more accurately, through all the stress, pressure, financial challenges, etc., that make for a modern-day life, I never stopped loving learning.

Here in the US, I started out by working a very intense 8–10 months for a dynamic and entrepreneurial start-up marine chartering and marine operating company. Sadly, the company did not make it.

Next, I worked for eight years for a leading top-side ship repair company in Houston, Texas.

During these early years in the US, our family endured our fair share of what we jokingly called IT—immigration torture—issues, including inevitable delays following the tragic 9/11 attacks. Fortunately, we prevailed. We are blessed to be citizens of the USA now. And, for speechwriters, this is great personal-life-story material.

Finally, still based in Houston, I worked another eight years for a global company (headquartered in Finland) manufacturing marine and power plant reciprocating engines and other integrated engineering products, as well as providing lifecycle services to take care of all this equipment. In this marvelous organization (easily the best I have ever worked for) I was exposed to a breathtaking diversity and depth of engineering talent. Here, I came to have a high regard for Finland, especially for their engineers, and for their "sisu" culture, that admirable combination of guts and stamina in the face of adversity. It was not one bit surprising for me to discover that Finland's educational system is consistently ranked amongst the best of the best. Finland certainly does a lot of things right. It was a wonderful and broadening experience. I also developed an abiding admiration and respect for the few Swiss, Dutch, German, and Italian engineers I worked with. They are very good engineers indeed. We all see things differently, yet we all see them the same. This was an all-new experience. I soaked it in.

Inevitably, over 17 years of working in the US, I ended up managing many projects—pretty intense and challenging ones—with tons of pressure. Some were spectacularly difficult—fortunately, we consistently prevailed.

About six years ago, following company strategy and guidelines, my Finnish boss instructed me to get a Project Management Professional (PMP) qualification/certificate. This was now a global organizational requirement. I signed up for a project management course and started attending the Houston Chapter Project Management Institute (PMI-H) monthly meetings.

It was at one of these chapter meetings that I became aware of the PMI-Houston sponsored Toastmasters International clubs. I signed on immediately. My Toastmasters home club is the North Houston Project Managers Toastmasters. Once again, putting modesty aside, I can report that this club is an incredible crucible for leadership. Serendipitously, I began one of the most rewarding voyages of my later years. I began a voyage of public speaking. For those who are not familiar with Toastmasters International, it is a global organization with a mission to develop its members' leadership and communication skills, through the avenue of public speaking.

Speaking always makes me feel connected to my father in a very special way. Writing speeches forces me to read and research extensively. Public speaking has made me keenly aware that we all owe each other a duty of care, an argument I frequently articulate. Public speaking makes me learn, over and over again, that we are all like each other much more than we are different from each other. I particularly love the athlete Steve Prefontaine's quote, *"To give anything less than your best ... is to sacrifice the gift."* I feel deeply obligated to give my very best whenever I am granted the opportunity to speak in public. In the domain of public speaking, energy, enthusiasm, and excellence merge, creating alchemy like no other.

Perhaps inevitably, I began to sense that there has to be more to life than working out a career in a corporation. I felt an itch, a calling to do more—a heck of a lot more—with myself, with my life. Dear reader, don't tell me that you haven't ever felt this too—I just won't believe you; I just won't. Deep inside of me, I want to be a builder. I began to know, from deep down, that I had an imminent decision to make. I was confronting a "now or never" decision.

Quotes like this one by financier and philanthropist David Rubenstein began to resonate and sting simultaneously: *"If you're happy to sit at your desk and not take any risks you'll be sitting at your desk for the next 20 years."* If there were a contest called "words that slap," these words would be in contention for a medal!

My son had completed his education (an electrical engineer, YOO HOO!) and had gotten his first job. I spoke to him about my choices, my dilemma, and my increasingly louder inner callings. His beautiful response: "Hey, Dad ... go for it!"

I was still attached to, still very loyal to my splendid company, and knew that walking away would not be without consequences. A previous boss (a mentor too, a person I hugely admire) had once unequivocally and bluntly told me this: "In the final analysis, you must always do what is best for Rashid, and I will always support that." Thank you, Sir!

I discussed the option of leaving the corporate world with my wife and family. As always, they 100% supported me, but we were all achingly aware that I was seriously contemplating walking away from a marvelous company, a sure thing (to the extent that a job is a sure thing these days), a good income, and a comfortable life. I would be doing this in my mid-50s. This was not without considerable risk.

I was still vacillating. A company internal reorganization finally triggered my risky decision to leave corporate life. I would commit to an independent and entrepreneurial voyage; the nothing ventured, nothing gained type of thing.

This company reorganization, perhaps like some others, across other organizations, was, in my humble and unsolicited opinion, ill-conceived, made in an ivory tower, thousands of miles and a continent away. Important decisions were made with insufficient foresight, zero discussion, and insufficient local information, by remote, newly minted bosses, who I respectfully and kindly judge to be adequately capable and partially clueless. These ill-conceived decisions were subsequently enforced by local bosses who I respectfully and kindly judge as having ought to have known better; bosses who may well have spoken up persuasively and courageously if they were more practiced and accomplished public speakers and leaders—if they were more like my father, my gold standard. There is a big difference between managers and leaders. Obedience had trumped eloquence. Yes, public speaking is a surefire enabler of many necessary and good things, especially leadership.

And yet I would be remiss to not acknowledge my own accountability, perhaps even culpability in all this. I would like to think I was an excellent contributor and leader, generally respected and admired. I befriended every single work colleague I met or saw. My lessons from my sailing days were with me every day.

When making critical team, project or organizational decisions, my first and last question to myself was, "Would

I take this same decision if it were my very own company ... my precious company and my precious legacy bequeathed to me by generations of ancestors?" This is the only way I know to give my best, to not sacrifice the gift of the good life that I have been granted. In good conscience I can say I consistently put my company and team first.

My projects were usually well delivered; frequently they were flawlessly delivered. Putting modesty aside yet again, I was good at this stuff; I thrived under the pressure cooker conditions of difficult projects. I always sought out the best of the best engineers for my projects. Minimum qualification: Lead engineer has to be much smarter than me. I would use all my persuasion and planning skills, all my political acumen, and significant amounts of political capital to secure the best engineers for my projects.

I consistently maintained good relationships with all colleagues, but especially with "resource owners." I count some of them as special friends, who rightly and instinctively understood that we are in this together, that we swim or sink together, and that we are bound, even entangled, together by a duty of care. Martin Luther King Jr. articulated this superbly: *"We are all caught in an inescapable network of mutuality. Whatever affects one directly, affects all indirectly."* My all-time favorite project management lesson learned comes from a NASA web page: *"The project manager who is the smartest man on his project has done a lousy job of recruitment."* I couldn't agree more.

http://www.nasa.gov/offices/oce/llis/imported_
content/lesson_1956.html

Customers respected, liked, and admired my brilliant team members and yours truly—and it must be said, frequently hinted that I should join them. I diplomatically and firmly shut down all such conversations.

I truly did love being a part of my unique company, its exemplary diversity, and its engineering prowess. I continue to admire and greatly respect the organization. While there, I spearheaded an initiative to start a Toastmasters club in this company with the express objective of doing my bit, my duty of care, to make this a "great place to work" company. I even managed, behind the scenes, to contribute toward getting a Toastmasters club going in Vaasa, Finland, though sadly not in the company itself.

Despite all the above, I must face this: Perhaps I was not such a valuable asset, after all. I would be remiss to pretend otherwise. I will never truly know. The company is doing just fine, and life goes on splendidly—as always.

Either way, I told my bosses I would be departing, gave them plenty of time to look for a replacement and made every attempt to take care of my now department-less team. Some efforts were made to persuade me to reconsider, but I could not see real value for either company or me in staying on. There was a fundamental mismatch between the company's restructuring process, and aspirations of employees like myself. Me being moved away from my core competencies, strengths and passions, was suboptimal for both parties. Being accommodated and drawing unearned income were not attractive options for me. Our parting was amicable, perhaps exemplary.

I must again acknowledge my own shortcoming here, my flat-out failure, actually. If I were an even more skilled speaker and persuader, (I am a vastly improved speaker, and yes a good speaker, but as this instance proves, not good enough. I have more work to do.) I would have succeeded in persuading my bosses that they made the wrong decision regarding closing down my department.

One way to achieve and live by high standards—our sacred

duty to provide first-class feedback, to all, including bosses, with a good heart, without undue timidity, without getting fired or sidelined, and without getting disliked, despised or feared in the process—is to become a world-class speaker. Dear reader, I submit to you, we owe these high standards to our organizations and ourselves; or more accurately, we owe these high standards to each and every colleague in our organization. And, even at the risk of seeming delusional and grandiose, we owe these high standards to every person on the planet. Committing, right now, to becoming a world-class speaker is one heck of a good decision! Make it now!

I have deliberately made this company-departure story quite detailed to make a point. Life-altering events like this will happen to everyone—and **they provide excellent material for personal-life stories.** Whenever we are having a hard day, a bad time, we are being gifted with personal-story-material. With training and grittiness, public speakers and storytellers become experts at capturing and articulating these experiences; they "storify" and store them.

If, when your inevitable life-altering career event strikes, you simply have to feel sorry for yourself, go for it, go through it, and get it over with and done. Life-altering career disruptions happen to all, and will happen with increasing frequency to engineers and project managers. Dear reader, you know this just as well as I do; don't pretend otherwise. Get used to it. After you are done with your pity party, **convert it to a story.** It is entirely worthwhile to be able, at some point, to laugh at the way things eventually turn out. Things usually turn out for the best, anyway. There is a Yiddish joke: *"Do you know how to make God laugh? Tell him your plans."*

Here is EXERCISE # 2. Start a story file and begin collecting your life stories in them. Make a separate failure file, too.

Make a life timeline. Your personal stories, especially (self-deprecating) failures, will connect you to your audiences like nothing else. A disclosure—not making a story file for more than five years is the single biggest mistake I have made over my public speaking voyage.

To see an example of this, (converting a disruptive life event into a story) listen to Craig Valentine, who—in my opinion—is one of the best storytellers in the world. Go to Craig Valentine's website and check out the video on the home page: http://www.craigvalentine.com

Or this one: https://www.youtube.com/watch?v=obS8KY9zYMA&list=PLOUOKnL3iJ6CleE8bU6hmF9XfGPnSbMfb

This marvelous example can serve as a North Star for your future public speaking voyages.

My *second wish* for you is this: Someday, may your career-changing stories, publically delivered, be as enchanting, entertaining, motivating and inspiring as Craig Valentine's.

Ultimately, I made some firm personal decisions:

1. I will take a 9-month sabbatical from my career.
2. I will make this (department closure) the best thing that ever happened to me.
3. I will burn no bridges, but will burn the boats—thereby precluding the option of a return voyage. I shall not return to this company. It is essential for me to get into a "prevail or perish" mindset to do what I must in the next stage of my life.
4. My colleagues will forever be remembered as dear friends for life. They are wonderful people.
5. I will write a book. Why? Because the best way to become acquainted with a subject, or to become an expert in it, is to write a book about it. Hat tip to Benjamin Disraeli for reminding us of this. To which

I could add: A good way to become thoroughly acquainted with a subject is to write and give a speech about it.

6. For the duration of my sabbatical, I will work on creating and building something that is unique and valuable.
7. I will learn like a maniac. I will read at a ferocious pace.
8. I will live a super-healthy and thoroughly disciplined life for these 9 months.
9. I will not dwell on, nor worry about finances; confident that I will neither starve nor be evicted. I will focus relentlessly on the work and the opportunity. One way or another, struggle and all, we will survive. I will emerge from this OK. Financial headaches will be there, plenty of them no doubt, waiting patiently for me, at the end of the sabbatical!
10. I will never ever regret this decision.
11. I will never forget, for even a second, that I am a truly fortunate man.

This, dear reader is my life story—so far. It is a story of a fortunate man who still has much to do in a world in which there is much to be done.

Phase 1—Childhood & Education
Phase 2—The life of a marine engineer at sea
RESET
Sabbatical: higher studies.
Phase 3—The life of a manager in corporate and industrial USA
RESET
Sabbatical: In progress

Phase 4—Yet to be written.

I hope you feel you know me a little better now. Go ahead and admit it: I'm probably not that different from you. We are all in the same boat together. We all breathe the same air.

Interests and passions, comments on controversial topics and final thoughts

To round out this chapter, perhaps I should add a few more points:

Point One. Reading has been one of the great loves of my life. As a very young child I read any number of books, especially Enid Blyton books. I read consistently through my school and college days. I did not read much when sailing on ships, but made up between voyages. I read Sherlock Holmes and Agatha Christie mysteries compulsively.

I stopped reading entirely after I started working in the USA. This was a huge decade-long mistake! A huge life regret. It is recorded in my "failure file." It was while doing a course for project management certification that I heard other students constantly referring to the books they were reading. This got me back into the groove. After getting a Kindle, my reading pace took flight. I was back on track. I never go anywhere without my iPad now, and more than seventy-five percent of my iPad time is on the Kindle app. I have read about 40-50 books (almost all non-fiction) a year over the past few years, and hope to keep up this pace for the rest of my days.

If, like me, you feel you would be better off recapturing your motivation to read extensively, listen to Craig Valentine's "Read" / Bookstore story.

http://www.craigvalentine.com/20storiestall

Listen to story #20.

Additionally, here's a proverb that may catalyze your decision to start reading again: *"Those who do not read are no better off than those who cannot."*

Point Two. Like most males all over the world I was entranced, even addicted to sports, and did not care a hoot about politics. From my earliest school days I always participated in all sports—and I still exercise (mainly running) regularly. My plan is to jog more than 1,000 kilometers every year. The centenarian marathon runner Fauja Singh, now global icon, has been a huge inspiration for me. No more excuses!

We are all counseled to steer clear of politics, religion, and sex. Let me, with more chutzpah than common sense, touch on each of these and get them permanently out of the way. By the way, chutzpah means shameless audacity, even impudence. I beg your indulgence.

My serious interest in politics surfaced around the same time I started my public speaking voyage. I'd like to think I have a healthy irreverence for all politics. I do not think too reverently (nor disrespectfully) of political parties or politicians. When I sometimes hear politicians being described as charming rogues, or some inevitable combination of charming and rogue, I can't help but smile. My interest in politics is not so much about politics, or policy, or politicians and their positions; rather it is about the skills and techniques which politicians (and their teams) use in messaging and communicating. This intrigues me, brings out the wannabe detective in me. What are they really up to? What are they really doing to win votes? In my judgment, the politicians who usually win are the ones who appear better spoken, the ones who appear more confident, and the ones who tell the best stories. It is a worrying late-in-life conclusion, but I have reached this conclusion anyway.

I do not agree with those elements of prevalent culture that class all politicians as being unrepentantly self-centered; or the Monday-morning-quarterback culture that feels entitled to suspect every politician's every move, and to disrespect them by default. While politicians are certainly no saints, and never will be, I judge them to be individuals who are willing to take on significant challenges, and live with levels of uncertainty and ambiguity that many of us could not bear. This, I respect and admire.

For me, these two quotes by (or at least ascribed to) Winston Churchill, former prime minister of the United Kingdom, best capture the realities and frailties of political systems, and inform my present thinking: *"Democracy is the worst form of government, except for all the others,"* and, *"The inherent vice of capitalism is the unequal sharing of blessings; the inherent virtue of socialism is the equal sharing of miseries."* I think these best explain the inexorable forward march of representative democracies and capitalist economies. It will be a good day indeed when dictators, tyrants, and other non-democracies are relics of a never-to-be-forgotten past.

I read this in *Profiles in Courage* by John F. Kennedy and I fundamentally endorse the argument: *For in a democracy, every citizen, (including those who do not vote, those who take no interest in Government, those who have only disdain for the politician and the profession), 'holds office'; every one of us is in a position of responsibility; and, in the final analysis, the kind of government we get depends on how we fulfill those responsibilities. We the people, are the boss, and we will get the kind of political leadership, be it good or bad, that we demand and deserve.*

That's my thinking on politics: I shall discuss politics no further.

By religion, I am a Zoroastrian, commonly called a Parsee in the Indian subcontinent. I feel firmly connected to my religion, and will always faithfully belong to it. I feel forever blessed to be born into it. I do not feel self-conscious, superior, or inferior about my religion. I simply accept it as a part of my life. Yet, without any doubt, I am not destined to ever win accolades, prizes, or medals for being super-religious or super-spiritual. If my religion has to be summed up in six words, here they are *"Good Thoughts. Good Words. Good Deeds."* Good enough for me. This is a North Star that guides me.

And here is another North Star that guides me, this one from the world of breathtaking oratory—with some modifications.

With a good conscience my only sure reward, with legacy and history the final judge of my deeds, let me go forth and live, and lead, in the lands I love, asking His blessing and His help, but knowing that here on earth God's work must truly be my own.

Simultaneously, and there's no way I can deny this either: I fearlessly, routinely, and silently, thank God for Secularism. I don't want to even imagine a world without it.

That's it on religion: I shall discuss religion no further.

Sex. Oh well: Here's something I read in a book called *Speak Like Churchill, Stand Like Lincoln* by James C. Hume. I request a chutzpah allowance from you:

At the Other Club in London, new members are initiated by having to deliver an extemporaneous talk on a subject picked randomly from a hat.

When it came time for Churchill to be initiated, the chairman reached into the hat and pulled out a card that had on it a single word: "SEX."

Churchill looked at the card and intoned in measured tones, "Sex ... (pause) ... it gives me great pleasure."

Then Churchill sat down.

Enough said! If you smiled or laughed—well, we aren't all that different!

And moving forward, please, please, never again start your

speeches with "It gives me great pleasure ..."

That's it with sex: I shall discuss sex no further.

Final comments now:

The public figure (who has lived and led during my lifetime) I most admire is Nelson Mandela. One of my favorite books is *Long Walk to Freedom*, especially chapter 115. Wannabe world leaders—this chapter is compulsory reading for you! Please read, and re-read, and re-read yet again. I dare you to come close!

As a newish citizen of the USA, I am interested in, and committed to, doing my bit toward making this "a more perfect union." Putting modesty aside, I think I do a good job with this one.

I admire people who long to build, push boundaries, set breathtaking targets, and never become egomaniacs.

I prefer to stay away from, yet never disrespect, human beings who feel entitled to constantly complain and criticize, and who feel entitled to their negative energy. I resolutely and decently steer clear of folk who feel entitled to smug superiority, and worse, contempt for others.

I harbor a healthy mistrust of the satisfying purity of indignation and outrage. Equanimity is a preferable option.

I'll confess to frequently wishing that people and peoples would be a little bit more "neurotically rational" a little more often. Hey, I am an engineer; this mindset goes with the turf.

I'll close with this. I am my parents' son. My father lives inside of me. I am an ambassador for all that they and my ancestors have stood for. I am a fortunate man.

I will never forget that there are more than seven billion people on our planet. The poorest one billion live in conditions wretched beyond description. There's no getting away from this, and no forgetting this: For every one citizen living in the US, there are three human beings on this planet who live in indescribable conditions of deprivation. The poorest two billion (that's six for every one US citizen) may, unimaginably, never know a glass of clean drinking water or a sanitation facility. How can I not be relentlessly grateful, unyieldingly thankful? I can never forget, and cannot be allowed to forget—I've been a truly fortunate man.

I'd like to live the rest of my life abiding by certain guidelines, certain principles. Like Mahatma Gandhi, *I resolve to fear no person on earth, and to bear ill will towards no person on earth.* The "no fear" part of this can get super-tough: Attempt pragmatically with caution, wisdom, street smarts, sound judgment, and yes, some daredevilry. Like Abraham Lincoln, I want to live *with malice towards none and with charity for all.* This is not all that tough: We can all do it. Like John F. Kennedy, I want to remain *an idealist without illusions.* This is doable, too. Like Martin Luther King, Jr., I will *refuse to accept despair as the final response to the ambiguities of human history and human folly.* Giving in to despair on a temporary, strictly short-term basis is sort of acceptable, sort of unavoidable.

I know, in a non-negotiable way, that we are all in the same boat together. I know, in a non-negotiable way, that we all cherish our children's futures. I like the way Sting expressed this in his TED Talk: *The fact is, whether you're a rock star, or whether you're a welder in a shipyard, or a tribesman in the upper Amazon, or the queen of England, at the end of the day, we're all in the same boat.* Spot on!

I know that wishing others well is always an option, and it is always a "common interest."

So, dear reader, let me wish you well with an ancient maritime blessing. "May God bless you ... and all who sail with you."

Enough! Indeed, more than enough about me!

Thank you for voyaging with me through this chapter.

You're welcome to attempt an optional exercise now. Convert this deliberately long narrative into a 600-word speech. Go ahead; give it a shot. I didn't say it's easy, but it's really not that tough either.

Now, start writing your story, even if this means writing only an initial word; before proceeding to the next chapter. Just start. This exercise, thoroughly completed, will provide endless raw material for every speech you ever need to write or give. If you do not start, candidly, you are shorting yourself. And this is just chapter 1. And I intend to negotiate hard with you all the way.

Chapter 2

Who Are You?

"Imagination is more important than knowledge."
— Albert Einstein

"Who are you?" I cannot knowledgably answer this question. But with imagination I can profile an ideal reader, one who will truly benefit from this book. To the extent that you can identify with this profile, this book has been written for you.

I'll confess, and I ask your indulgence: I view myself only partially as an author. Partially, I envision this book to be a full-fledged product, created by a drive and desire to provide something unique and valuable—and to fill a gap, a hole, that I inadvertently stumbled into.

I will state an opinion upfront, perhaps an unwelcome one. It is one that has been reinforced repeatedly along the way. I do not believe anyone can become an expert public speaker and storyteller by reading only one book, no matter how well-known or skilled the author, or no matter the claims of the author. Yes there are many wonderful and complete books out there, but after reading a whole lot of them, I can report that I find them all to have sufficiently unique offerings.

I envision you returning to this book repeatedly over a period of two to four years. After you first read this book, (almost certainly an elementary or inspectional read) I envision you re-reading this book, analytically and syntopically—along with the many other books (and products) cited and recommended in *Necessary Bridges*.

I envision us making an agreement, a deal, a quasi-contract.

My part of the deal is this: I commit to providing you with building blocks, guidance, direction, and tools. I commit to sharing my journey's lessons learned, even ones that appear to have no direct bearing on public speaking and storytelling, so that your learning is more rapid than mine was. I commit to keeping you motivated and on track as you undertake this voyage. This is far and away my most important commitment, and the one I will struggle with most. The book's content will be contextualized by a knowledge and passion for project management and engineering. The content will, in equal measure, be contextualized by a passion for and a knowledge of public speaking and storytelling. My deliverables are contained in the pages of this product. I have to keep pushing you.

Your bit of the bargain is this: You must commit to being a dedicated learner, preferably an expert student, and an enthusiastic practitioner—user of the product.

This is non-negotiable. Without this commitment from both sides, success can hardly be assured. Without such commitment, you may learn a little bit intellectually about public speaking and storytelling, but I want to negotiate for far more than that. Here, we the parties to this agreement are gauging each other. I would like you, without equivocation, without nuance, to know my expectations. You must commit.

If you flat-out refuse to commit, I respectfully recognize and regretfully acknowledge that this would be a good time for you to take *Necessary Bridges* and throw it into the sea. It is like procuring a product that you have no intention of using.

Viewed in this light, you, the reader, are my direct customer, and I, the author, am your direct supplier or vendor. As your vendor, first and foremost, I must know your needs. Next I must provide, at a very minimum, a value equivalent to the price of this book to you, my customer.

So who are you? Perhaps you fall into one or more of these categories:

1. You are an engineer, or a project manager, or both.
2. You are not yet, but you aspire to be an engineer, or a project manager, or both.
3. You are currently a student of engineering, or project

management, or both.

4. You have interest in public speaking and storytelling—as a competency that can help you become a more rounded and upwardly mobile professional. You want to learn more, to give it a try. You are willing to commit.

5. You aspire to progress professionally and personally in life. You acknowledge that continuous improvement is essential to achieve this aspiration. You are willing to step beyond the disciplines, confines, and structure of Project Management and Engineering, toward realizing these aspirations.

6. You may be a Toastmaster, or a public speaker, or a storyteller who likes to learn more about these skills, or simply to read books on these topics.

7. You may even be a presentation or speaking coach with engineers and project managers amongst your clients—and want to better understand this occasionally strange breed of professionals. You may even confess to having thought: "How can these smart, smart, folk, project managers and engineers, be so disconnected and disinterested—dare I say clueless—about something as simple and essential as public speaking and storytelling? Wow, I have an interesting challenge! Bring it on!"

If you fall into any of these categories, then your needs fall into my sights, my core competence, and with your permission, I would love to push you onward to excellence in public speaking and storytelling. I ask to be your preferred vendor, your supplier of choice. Fair enough?

Three stories now. If these events had not occurred, if these conversations had not taken place, this book would not have been written. These are the events that made me realize that engineers and project managers are not helping themselves by not committing to acquiring expertise in public speaking and storytelling. These incidents convinced me that we engineers and project managers have a shortcoming that requires remedy.

Story 1: Years ago in a Toastmasters meeting, a young engineer came up to me and said "Rashid, I wish I could get you to speak to groups of engineers more often. I know they will connect with you." There is always a relentlessly supportive atmosphere in my Toastmasters clubs, so I took this comment with a pinch of salt and good grace—and thought nothing more of it. We Toastmasters are constantly complementing and pushing one another. Kind and sincere comments are ubiquitous. But I was a bit puzzled by the comment and perhaps that is why I remembered it.

Story 2: Once, at work, I asked one of my project engineers, a brilliant man, to stop by at a vendor's location and pick up a finished product. I liked the vendor and was friendly with him. Somehow this brilliant engineer took a dislike to the vendor, (at least, that's what I suspect happened) and what seemed like a truly simple task did not get done. This became a puzzle to me. I did not then appreciate how seriously some engineers sometimes lack communication skills, leadership skills, or people skills. I was unable to understand how this utterly simple task got complicated. I presumed back then, that by default, everyone had fundamental people, communication, and leadership skills, just like I did. Slowly and disbelievingly, I discovered that this was not always so.

Story 3: Sometime ago, as part of my learning and development, I requested a 360 feedback survey from an external management association. My company agreed and I had the survey done.

For readers unfamiliar with 360 surveys, this is worth

spending some time on. A 360 survey provides feedback from multiple people in an employee's work environment, including subordinates, peers, and supervisors, as well as the employee. If you have never had one of these, allow me to recommend that you take immediate steps to get one for yourself.

One purpose of this survey is to uncover the difference in the way candidates view themselves, vis-à-vis the way their colleagues view them. When the gap between these viewpoints is small, it is good; it reveals that the candidate being 360-evaluated has emotional intelligence. When the gap is large, there is room for improvement, especially when the candidate holds the vastly superior viewpoint.

Anyway, my 360-evaluation went well. At the end of the process, there was a debriefing session by a facilitator. It was a part of the telephone conversation with my facilitator that has long stayed with me.

The written summary of my survey was nice: *"Results show that you are high in the influence style ... Your results are most positive and indicate that you are viewed as effective in your current role."* There was plenty of good commentary in the same vein. Understandably, I was pleased with the results, and I made good note of all the recommendations.

When closing the process, during the final debriefing, I had a very nice telephone conversation with the facilitator. Truthfully, it was a splendid and detailed conversation, over an hour and I enjoyed it tremendously. Toward the end she asked me: "Rashid, are you sure that you are an engineer?" I wasn't sure I understood the question. Obviously I was an engineer— for decades. I said "Yes," and probed as to why she asked an obvious question. She responded: "I have never spoken to an engineer quite like you. I wish I could have someone like you along with me when debriefing or training other engineers."

Completely surprised, and partially confused, I asked her

to explain further. She said in general, in these surveys, the data suggests that disproportionately, engineers have a much higher opinion of themselves than their non-engineer peers do, and many engineers seem incapable (or disinclined) of detecting or understanding when they have created an upset or an emotionally disruptive issue. They simply do not sense that they are out of tune with others. They do not understand why others get upset with, or disagree with their clearly stated and obvious facts. Indeed they are astonished that others "don't get it." They feel entitled to, and are sometimes even smugly satisfied with, their worldview. Now of course these weren't her exact words; they were far gentler and kinder, and far more diplomatic. Nonetheless this is how I remember the conversation; what I took away from it after reading between the lines.

I was again disbelievingly beginning to grasp that just because I got along terrifically with my engineer and non-engineer colleagues, I was wrong in presuming that all engineers got on equally well with their non-engineer colleagues. We engineers are seldom shining starts of emotional intelligence. If you are an engineer and this comes to you as a surprise— well you have plenty of company.

I suddenly recalled an incident from well over a decade ago, when a role model and adroit boss yelled at me, very publically, "Mr. Rashid! You are the most stubborn man I have ever come across! You never listen to anyone!" Yep, I've been there. I distinctly remember being puzzled by this dressing down. I simply didn't get that I was rough-riding over others, and was blissfully unaware of the consequences of my approach. When I mentioned the incident to my wife, she concurred with the gold standard for clarity and brevity: "Exactly!"

I must add a comment about this boss. He was a masterful practitioner of the "A leader never loses his temper except deliberately at the place and time of his choosing, in order to achieve a specific purpose" approach, and he nailed it that day. We both knew exactly what he was pulling off, and pull it off he did. I had nothing left to do but thank him.

The conversation with the 360-facilitator marked a turning point of sorts, an explicit recognition. I had to acknowledge a gap in the skills and training of engineers. Yes, I was slowly and surely concluding, **"There is a mismatch between what engineers think they need to know and learn, and with what they really need to know and learn."** While this mismatch is initially subtle and not noticeable, it becomes more obvious as they advance professionally.

Unaddressed, this mismatch can and may well cripple engineers' careers. I would be remiss to state this less bluntly, or more diplomatically. It is worth repeating: Unaddressed, this mismatch can and may well cripple engineers' careers. And sadly, the odds increase that more senior engineers will become more angry, even cynical, or bitter, or twisted— especially when youngsters become their bosses. I had seen this at sea, and I've seen it ashore. It is not a good place for anyone, let alone great engineers.

I frequently heard self-deprecating and engineer deprecating humor from the few engineers who spoke in Toastmasters clubs, followed by knowing laughter from the audience. It's one thing to have a little good-spirited fun, but it is quite another thing to believe that there is factual basis for such laugh lines. Further, in the public speaking world, I was exposed to some excellent laugh lines targeting engineers; for instance: "Marketing proposes A. Sales responds with B. Manufacturing argues back with C. *(They seem to argue all the time.)* Management intones D. Business analysts pontificate E. And engineering—oh well … engineers … will they ever learn how to speak?"

So there seems to be an opinion out there that engineers cannot speak. I for one, putting on my "neurotically-rational" hat, do not accept this nonsense for a second. However, I could no longer ignore this widely held wrong opinion.

I ran into a similar puzzle, or should I say mystery, with project managers.

Over the past six years I have gone for many Project Management Institute-Houston (PMI-H) meetings and some larger conferences. Well over half the talks are about soft skills, with speakers routinely evangelizing communication and leadership. Leadership and communication skills are acknowledged as essential to executing successful projects. There is no debate left. This discussion is over.

In general leadership, communication, and presentation training is not inexpensive—and is a one-time experience. For the more fortunate it may be an annual experience.

There are alternates to these more expensive and less frequent specialized trainings, which are the PMI-Houston sponsored Toastmasters clubs. These clubs are specifically set up to allow and encourage project management terminology and jargon in meetings and speeches. For economy, nothing comes close. The program is self-paced. The education program has a proven success record—for decades. These are excellent clubs and would benefit any project manager committed to self-improvement. I've said it before and I will say it again: These PMI-H sponsored Toastmasters Clubs are crucibles for leadership.

Trivia: Crucibles are vessels medieval alchemists used in their attempts to turn base metals into gold.

Here's the puzzle: There are more than 4,000 members in the PMI-Houston chapter. All 4,000 are aware that they can only benefit by being practiced leaders and communicators. Yet only 1% of the chapter members are Toastmasters in the sponsored clubs. To me, this remains a puzzle, a mystery.

A common observation: Too many project managers, especially recently promoted ones, still think having outstanding technical ability is the most important asset to have as project leader. Wrong! While I do not condone or accept technical illiteracy, it is time to move on. And in growing as a project manager, public speaking and storytelling is a phenomenal lever. And, if you as project manager are the smartest person on your team, you have done a terrible job with recruitment!

Again, I see a mismatch. In some ways it is similar to the mismatch relating to engineers. **"There is a mismatch between what project managers know that they need to excel at, and with what they commit to excelling at."** By commit, I mean time and money. I do not know many ways of committing to anything without simultaneously committing both time and money.

At a PMI-Houston conference, I heard this beautifully articulated by keynote speaker Rory Vaden: *"My pastor once told me that if you want to know what a person really believes in then you don't need to waste time asking them. Instead just look at their calendar and their checkbook; because what we spend our time and our money on is what we truly value most."* Well said!

Dear reader, if any of the above sounds familiar, even distressingly familiar, or resonates with you, then now is the time to commit. Take your first step onto a *Necessary Bridge*. Commit to becoming an expert public speaker and storyteller.

The gulf between the islands of project management and engineering, and the islands of public speaking and storytelling, is way too wide. It is time to build *Necessary Bridges*. This product aims to be one such bridge. And, yours truly, the creator of this product, intends to evangelize public speaking and storytelling to any and all project managers and engineers who will listen. Indeed, I argue that public speaking and storytelling should be an integral part of the curriculum of project management and engineering undergraduate and graduate course work. And giving a short speech and telling one story should be an essential part of any job interview for project managers and engineers.

Archimedes famously said, "Give me a lever long enough, and a fulcrum, and I shall move the world." Allow me to evangelize: "If you want to move up in your world, public speaking and storytelling expertise can be your career scaling lever."

Very recently, in a corporate Toastmasters meeting, I heard a seasoned toastmaster tell a story. I subsequently interviewed her and asked her for permission to use it.

Almost two decades ago, she had just migrated from China to the USA and got a good job in the oil and gas industry. English was her second language. She was technically very skilled at her work, and was doing an excellent job. But she felt reticent, inhibited, and seldom spoke or participated in team meetings.

Her work was described as very detailed and excellent. Yet her first annual performance review did not go as well as she expected.

She was surprised.

She was told: "Your technical skills are superb; your work output is excellent. However, to navigate upwards in our organization is a lot like riding a bicycle with a front wheel and a back wheel. The back wheel is the engine; it moves the bike, it is the technical wheel and your wheel is very strong. However, to steer and set direction, you have to use the front wheel which is about communication and leadership. This wheel of yours is underdeveloped. Why don't you take some training courses in communication and leadership?"

This feedback served as a wake-up call and stayed with her through her career. She went on to take some communication, presentation, and leadership courses, but felt that the benefits were ephemeral. Ten years later she discovered Toastmasters. It was her diligent participation in Toastmasters that helped her the most.

Because, she discovered, like I have, that nothing, repeat nothing, parallels standing in front of and speaking to groups of people; often, regularly, frequently.

Toastmasters offers its members the stage time and a friendly environment to do so. She says her front wheel got bigger and stronger as she overcame her fear with confidence through practicing her speeches and taking on club leadership roles. She has, in her own way, been evangelizing public speaking and storytelling ever since.

She was fortunate that she was given this guidance very early on in her career, and she was very smart to immediately heed it and to act. Not all project managers and engineers will be so fortunate.

As a project manager and engineer, would you benefit from a similar performance review evaluation? Would it be true? Does your front wheel need some work? Remember, giving a tough performance evaluation is usually harder than receiving one: Your supervisor may not be up to it, or may not care enough. I ask you to be an idealist without illusions. Your supervisor may not be good enough to give you the evaluation you most deserve, or may not care enough.

I insist: Be an idealist without illusions. Your growth is your responsibility. If you are fortunate, your company will contribute to your growth, but this is not often the case.

If you would like to develop your front wheel too, and be in charge of setting your own direction, then your explicit commitment to excellence in public speaking and storytelling, coupled with this book, this product, can be the lever that moves your world.

And remember Rory Vaden's message: If you want to judge for yourself whether you have truly committed, then just look at your calendar and your checkbook; because what you spend your time and your money on, is what truly matters to you. Period.

So, returning to our opening question: "Who are you?"

1. Are you are an engineer or/and a project manager?
2. If no, do you eventually plan to become an engineer or/ and a project manager?
3. Do you aspire to progress in life professionally and personally?
4. Do you acknowledge that continuous improvement is the only way forward?
5. Are you willing to commit to doing the needful toward becoming a better public speaker and storyteller?
6. Will this commitment be reflected in your calendar and checkbook?
7. Are you a current Toastmaster, public speaker, or storyteller?
8. Are you currently a presentation skills coach or similar?

If the answer is yes to some or all of these questions, then we have a solid basis for working together—doing business together.

I read this in a book called *It's Your Time to Shine* by Sandra Zimmer, who has brilliantly coached me in the past. *"I believe the purpose of life is to grow and change so that we can be of greater service. I believe there is an innate desire in each human soul to make a contribution by giving his or her gifts to others."*

Do you agree with this? If yes, we have more than a solid basis for working together.

Let's proceed to define our responsibilities and tasks with a project management approach.

Chapter 3

Your Project Charter

"Vision without action is a daydream.
Action without vision is a nightmare."
— Japanese proverb

At the risk of being professionally and politically incorrect, I am assuming that since you are an engineer or project manager, you may have an above-average IQ. I am further assuming that you have made above-average academic efforts to get to where you are professionally. Is this correct? You have studied for long hours over long years. You have learned a lot about lots of things. You have successfully passed many exams and difficult exams. You've most likely made midlife and midcareer investments and sacrifices to keep progressing: especially if you're a certified Project Management Professional (PMP), or a certified Professional Engineer (PE). You are a good learner, a quick learner, and probably a thorough learner. Am I right? Your family is proud of your achievements and of the way you have persevered. As a result of all this, you have the good fortune of a decent income. You have excellent prospects for a financially successful future in a rapidly changing world. To summarize: Your IQ and your education are above average; your learning and knowledge are above average; and you are fortunate, i.e., you're in a good place in life. Am I right?

Here is something for you to consider. The body of knowledge for engineering is vast, indeed incomprehensibly vast. The body of knowledge for project management is not insignificant—but probably small compared to engineering. Now know this: the body of knowledge of public speaking and storytelling is, by comparison, miniscule.

For project managers and engineers to intellectually learn the body of knowledge of public speaking and storytelling is not an intellectual challenge. You will make the endeavor look easy, even embarrassingly easy. This is an advantage that we have. Let's be grateful and recognize the advantage of our talents and background. But let us not rest on our laurels.

If you read my story in chapter 1, you will recall that I spearheaded a move to start a Toastmasters club in my last company. Guess how many engineers and project managers are members of the club? Guess how many engineers and project managers from my team (they were my direct reports) are members? Guess how many of the very few who do attend meetings routinely speak? If you guessed "close to zero," you are right.

Yet I remain cautiously optimistic that I will eventually prevail. I have the better argument. Here it is. **Every project manager and engineer will be a significantly better project manager and engineer — simply by being an expert public speaker and storyteller, too.** Period. This is my argument, and I am right. This is not arrogance; please forgive me, and please believe me; this is confidence. Best of all, I am seeing more and more young engineers joining Toastmasters clubs.

Imagine that I have never tasted sugar (or salt, or spice), or anything sweet (or salty, or spicy); ever. Now tell me what sugar (or salt, or spice) tastes like. I'm not so sure you can. However you can encourage me to taste something sweet (or salty, or spicy), and then you can, more easily, describe to me what it tastes like. Does this make some sense? Any sense?

Once you commit to public speaking and storytelling excellence, once you get started on your public speaking and storytelling voyage, once you start public speaking regularly, once you dismiss the nonsense that engineers cannot speak, once you dismiss the nonsense that the fear of public speaking is greater than the fear of death, once you dismiss the nonsense that the project manager has to be the technically smartest person on the project, once you taste the sugar; the rewards are immediate. And our subsequent conversation will flow in both directions more easily—in all variations, sweet, salty, and spicy.

You will love the feeling of greater self-confidence and self-esteem. You will love the feeling that you are making a meaningful contribution. You will love the feeling of being granted the attention of an attentive audience, and the positive and generous feedback that follows. You will love the feeling of being your authentic self (the real, flawed, and vulnerable you), and being acknowledged for it. Most of all, you will love the feeling of connection with an audience that comes from truly sharing yourself, your experience, your stories, and your knowledge; of giving the best of yourself. You will love the taste of this sugar. And hopefully, after this happens for long enough, after you experience public speaking and storytelling long enough, you will join me in evangelizing public speaking and storytelling to project managers and engineers. Especially younger professionals and students. I intend to negotiate with you relentlessly for this.

My primary tasks, the ones I most want to accomplish, are: (1) to convince you to commit to public speaking and storytelling excellence (I know, I know … you think it is not really necessary. Well, you are wrong!) and (2) to keep you motivated (for the rest of your life) to never stop getting better. Look out for the asymptote approach toward expertise in a forthcoming chapter.

My secondary task is to provide content, i.e. the body of knowledge of public speaking and storytelling in an easy to digest and practical format. Additionally, I will provide exercises for you to complete, provide examples, and to point to external resources to take you beyond the fundamentals.

If my primary task is thoroughly accomplished, project managers and engineers will accomplish the secondary task (learning, absorbing and internalizing the content) with embarrassing ease.

I will now make a Project Charter for you to use as a sample. Here is your EXERCISE #3. I ask that you make your own Project Charter. Your own Project Charter will expedite your explicit commitments on your calendar and on your checkbook. This is what I am after: your written, explicit commitments of time and money. We are going nowhere without these commitments.

For those who need a quick refresher on project charters, here it is: *A project charter is a formal document recognizing the existence of a project. The project manager may create it, but it is to be issued by the sponsor in the initiating process.* (We may have to wink at this requirement, be a bit flexible, a bit creative, imaginative, unless you can rope in a sponsor, perhaps your supervisor.) *The project charter defines the high-level requirement for the project and links the project to other ongoing work.*

My Project Charter

A skills, and skills-perception gap has been detected within the professions of engineering and project management. This is a globally recognized issue. In order to address and correct this gap, "Powers-That-Be," the **sponsor**, has authorized a project with a budget not to exceed US $7,500. The project is to be **named** the **"Necessary Bridges"** project.

The project **scope**, i.e. the work of the project, is to create a product, in book form, that is to be distributed to practicing and aspiring project managers and engineers—hereafter referred to as PM&E.

The product is required to provide motivation, information, education, and direction for PM&E, with the **objective** of increasing PM&E commitment to, and expertise in public speaking and storytelling—hereafter referred to as PS&ST. It is acceptable for the product to demand high standards, and a high commitment to excellence from the product user.

Rashid N. Kapadia is appointed **Project Manager**. Project Manager is fully responsible for executing the project within budget. It is accepted and agreed that the Project Manager will not charge for his time or expertise. His efforts and expertise will be accepted by "Powers That Be" as a labor of love. Project Manager will not be provided any paid team members. He is authorized to accept assistance from volunteers, if he is able to enroll such volunteers, by his own efforts.

The project **deliverable** is a self-published book, available in e-book format, and in print format, ready for sale. The title of the book is to be: ***Necessary Bridges: Public Speaking & Storytelling for Project Managers & Engineers.***

The price for the e-book format is to be US $10. The price for the print version of the book is not to exceed US $25.

Timeline: The project is required to commence no later than July 1, 2014 and be completed by December 31, 2014.

High-level project plan: The book *A.P.E.: Author, Publisher, Entrepreneur—How to Publish a Book* by Guy Kawasaki and Shawn Welch is to be used as the Project Plan. Approximate pricing from external vendors is indicated in this document.

The project is expected to have three **phases**.

Phase 1 = Being an author and doing the work of an author.

Phase 2 = Being a publisher and doing the work of a publisher.

Phase 3 = Being an entrepreneur and doing the work of an entrepreneur.

Phases 1 and 3 are authorized for immediate commencement. Expenditure is authorized.

Phase 2 will be authorized after the Phase 1 deliverable has been reviewed by at least five people, preferably unpaid experts. If this review requirement causes some delays in final production, such delays will be accepted.

Budget: Estimate US $2,500 for each phase. Total project budget US $7,500.

Stakeholders:
- Rashid N. Kapadia as A.P.E. and Project Manager.
- All external vendors and suppliers—as detailed in Kawasaki-Welch book.
- 5 or more expert reviewers.
- Powers-That-Be, as Sponsor.

Not included in project scope:
Costs relating to marketing, distribution logistics, sales etc.—after book is published.

Signed—Powers-That-Be.
June 15, 2014

Now it is your turn—complete EXERCISE #3: Create your own project charter.

It does not need to be perfect; it does need to be "done." Done now is better than perfect later!

Your own Project Charter will expedite your explicit commitments on your calendar and on your checkbook. This is what we are after: your written, explicit commitments of time and money.

Here is my *third wish* for you. May you always be a successful project manager, successfully executing all your projects in scope, on time and within budget. And with top quality.

I read this in the Kawasaki-Welch book, A.P.E. *Develop the habit of citing sources. Give credit when others point you to something that you share. Acknowledge them by name. This shows that you have class and that you know how the game works. You'll also rack up karma points, so remember: ABC ("Always Be Crediting").* Excellent advice for speakers, too!

I bring this up because I know I came across this quotation some time ago, but I simply cannot remember where, or find the source—not even on Google! *It is harder to decide—really and truly decide—to become a millionaire, than it is to actually become a millionaire.* Determined to stay away from bad karma, I gratefully acknowledge the unknown source and ask that you now reflect on this message thoughtfully. A modified version of this very quote is a summary of this entire chapter. *It is harder to decide—really and truly decide—to become an expert PS&ST, especially for most PM&Es, than it is to actually become an expert PS&ST.* Once you decide to commit to PS&ST expertise, our highest hurdle is cleared. Calendar and checkbook entries in place? Life story writing started? Story file created? Failure file created? Sponsor on board? Project Charter signed?

Mindful of my dual responsibilities (1) getting reluctant PM&Es to—really and truly decide—to become excellent public speakers and storytellers and (2) providing content, direction, and information on the subject of PS&ST, I have chosen to structure a part of this book loosely based on the musical form known as rondo form. Here a principal theme alternates with something contrasting—like A-B-A-C-A-D-A.

An example would be:
- Ronald Reagan cut taxes and shrank government
- Ronald Reagan initially chose a career in entertainment
- Ronald Reagan cut taxes and shrank government

- Ronald Reagan was governor of California
- Ronald Reagan cut taxes and shrank government
- Ronald Reagan was president of USA
- Ronald Reagan cut taxes and shrank government

In the event you have not made your own project charter yet, this may help.

I will imagine that a young engineer and aspiring project manager has approached me and requested that I be a mentor. Let's use a unisex name, say Ash (as in Asher, or Ashley, or Ashlyn, or Ashton).

Now, let's imagine that I know, respect, and like Ash's parents. Our professional paths have crossed in the past. We are not really friends, more like acquaintances. Both of Ash's parents are PM&Es in solid, larger organizations. They are proud of their professions and are rock-solid ambassadors for these professions. They are delighted that Ash has chosen to follow in their footsteps. Sadly, their PS&ST skills are not where they should be. Let's not sugarcoat the issue. The PS&ST skills of too many PM&Es are not where they should be. Ash's parents know, and quietly acknowledge, that they have lowered their career ceiling as a consequence of lacking this skillset. Deep down they acknowledge that they lacked the self-discipline and gumption to dive into the world of PS&ST when they should have. It didn't seem necessary back then. And the thought of standing in front of an audience still brings on all the ubiquitous fears associated with public speaking. Looking back, they wish that more books like *Necessary Bridges* were available in their time. They wish that there were more PS&ST evangelists in their time. They are delighted that, despite inhibitions, Ash is diving in with gumption.

I feel honored to have been approached by Ash. There are few joys greater than mentoring willing young professionals.

We have a good laugh when Ash shares this Mark Twain quote with me. *"When I was a child of 14, my parents were so ignorant I could hardly stand to have them around. But when I got to be 21, I was astonished at how much they had learned in seven years."*

Ash has agreed to do this. It is actually a list of things I wish I had done at the very start of my public speaking voyage. I acknowledge it is a long list.

1. Join a Toastmasters club—preferably one that meets weekly. It is quite all right to miss a few meetings, especially when work comes in the way. Work comes first.
2. Commit to finishing the first 10 speeches (The Competent Communication manual) in 6–12 months.
3. Commit to finishing the first 10 leadership projects (The Competent Leader manual) in 12 – 18 months.
4. Commit to requesting a mentor from the Toastmasters club.
5. Commit to watching a minimum of one TED Talk every week.
6. Commit to listening to a minimum of two Moth stories every month.
7. Commit to watching or listening to one speech a month from the website *American Rhetoric—Top 100 speeches.* Ash's parents have said they would like to make this a monthly family ritual.
8. Read one book that I recommend every 30–90 days—some of these are not directly related to PS&ST.
9. Write one 18-minute TED Talk style speech in the first year.
10. Write one Moth StorySlam-style talk in the first or second year.
11. Present at work at every available opportunity—and

always get feedback after the presentation.
12. Commit to becoming an "expert student." More on this in another chapter.
13. Commit to attending one professional speaker's 2–3 day training event with keynotes and workshops—in the first 24 months. Ash's parents have agreed to finance this. They might even join Ash.
14. Take every presentation skills training available at work—paid for by the company.
15. Write down your life story in full detail in the first 12 months—no less than 5,000 words.
16. Make a story file and a failure file in the immediate future. One entry minimum per month into each file required.

Ash and I have agreed to speak for one hour every two months on the telephone—more frequently if required. I may attend Ash's Toastmasters club when Ash is speaking—once or twice a year.

I asked Ash and the parents to make a project charter. I also requested Ash's parents to write down their life stories in no less than 5,000 words.

Ash's Project Charter

My parents, who have tasked me with creating this project charter, are sponsors of this project. We have recognized that it is essential for me to begin acquiring public speaking and storytelling (hereafter referred to as PS&ST) expertise in the immediate future. We recognize that PS&ST is, unfortunately, not adequately encouraged at undergraduate, graduate, and early career development levels.

This charter establishes the existence of a four-year project to bring forth the speaker and leader that I intend to become. The name of the project is **Developing A Distinguishing Competency.**

The Project **Deliverables** are a DTM award and five professional level speeches.

Project **Scope** is to earn Toastmasters International's DTM (Distinguished Toastmaster) award in no more than four years, and to create no less than five (professional level) ready-to-deliver speeches. These may be in the form of keynote speeches, training presentations, TED Talk format speeches, Moth stories, entertaining speeches, or other project management and engineering (hereafter referred to as PM&E) related talks.

The project is to commence no later than January 2015. The 4-year **timeline** is to be divided into four phases, each phase being one year. A minimum of ten hours per month is my time commitment to this project. Any time used for (1) attending Toastmasters meetings, (2) preparing presentations for work, (3) delivering presentations at work, (4) speech writing, (5) watching TED Talks, (6) listening to Moth stories, (7) reviewing famous speeches, (8) reading PS&ST books, (9) studying PS&ST DVDs, mp3s, or CDs, (10) attending communication, leadership, or presentation (classroom or online) trainings, (11) evangelizing PS&ST at work, (12) volunteering at Toastmasters events, or (13) time spent with mentors, will count as project time.

Phase 1: (Year 1)
Complete the Competent Communicator requirements and get the CC certificate.
Phase 2: (Year 2)
Complete the Advanced Communicator Bronze requirements and get the ACB certificate.

Complete the Competent Leader and Advanced Leader Bronze requirements and get the CL and ALB certificates.
Complete one professional-level speech.
Phase 3: (Year 3)
Complete the Advanced Communicator Silver requirements and get the ACS certificate.
Complete the Advanced Leader Silver requirements and get the ALS certificate.
Complete two professional-level speeches.
Phase 4: (Year 4)
Complete the Advanced Communicator Gold requirements and get the ACG certificate.
Complete the High Performance Leadership (HPL) project requirements and get the DTM award.
Complete two professional-level speeches.

I (Ash) am appointed project manager. My supervisor has encouraged me to proceed and will support me by way of creating multiple presentation opportunities at work and will arrange for me to attend at least one company sponsored communication training every year.

The **budget** for the **Developing A Distinguishing Competency** project is a total of US $4,000, to be disbursed at US $1,000 per year. These funds are to be utilized for procuring resources and materials related directly to growth in PS&ST.

The **stakeholders** for the **Developing A Distinguishing Competency** project are my parents, my supervisor, my Toastmasters mentor, my other external mentors, and I.

Signed by project manager and project sponsors (Ash's Mom and Dad)

December 2014

Dear Reader, please do not proceed beyond this chapter without creating your own project charter. This may well be the first make-or-break point of your PS&ST voyage. This is the first step onto a *Necessary Bridge*.

Your part of the bargain is a commitment of time and money—explicitly expressed in your project charter. I believe 10 hours a month and US $1,000 a year for a minimum of two years is SMART (specific, measurable, action-oriented, relevant and time-bound). This may well prove to be the single best investment you ever make. Good Luck!

Here is my *fourth wish* for you:

As you set sail on your PS&ST voyage, may you be blessed with fair winds and following seas.

And may you someday evangelize PS&ST to young and upcoming PM&Es.

Chapter 4

To the Moon ... and ... to the Stars Beyond

"The greater danger for most of us lies not in setting our aim too high and falling short; but in setting our aim too low, and in achieving our mark."
— *Michelangelo*

The objective of this chapter is to ask you to aspire to a scorching, high standard in PS&ST expertise. Remember, you are an ambassador for one or two of the world's great professions. Nothing less will do. I also ask that you try your best to fall in love with PS&ST—whatever that means. Honor and respect that part within yourself (perhaps dormant now) that was born to speak, to share, and to tell stories.

Now that you have your commitment to PS&ST expertise in place—now that you have entries on your calendar *(a minimum two-year plan ... if you're not there yet ... renegotiate with yourself)* and commitments on your checkbook *(you have committed resources, yes money! And have a budget in place. How do you know the amount is enough? It must hurt a little, something must be sacrificed ... after all, this is your investment in upward-professional-mobility)*—let me raise the stakes one more time.

I ask you to believe in yourself, to trust yourself, and start preparing now for a day that may come: a day when you will be called upon to write and deliver a speech of immense consequence.

I insist that you imagine this vividly. Through your imagination, you now know that a day will come, even if it is decades away, when you will be called on to write and give a speech of immense importance. You must feel this in your body. If you do not feel any anxiety and/or exhilaration in your body, you are not imagining hard enough. Ideally the anxiety must be "just enough" to propel you upward and onward. If the anxiety is excessive, this too can be a good sign: it may be a sign that you already have an internal subconscious commitment, and this commitment is now finding its voice—and simultaneously setting off alarm bells—known in biology as the fight or flight response. More on this in a later chapter.

Your preparation toward this speech of immense consequence starts right now.

I am assuming you are in compliance with ALL requirements of the second paragraph of this chapter. If not, you can do better! If not, negotiate harder with yourself.

This chapter is about building the vision of yourself as a public speaker and storyteller. Look back at the quotation at the beginning of the previous chapter. Here is a variant of a similar quotation. Building the vision is as necessary as the action.

"Vision without action is merely a daydream. Action without vision just passes the time. Vision with action can change the world." — *Joel A. Barker*

I ask that you block out some uninterrupted time, 2–3 hours, and absorb the speech that follows in this sequence:

1. Read through the speech slowly and thoroughly, and absorb it intellectually. Take your time—but no interruptions.
2. Read some commentary and analysis of the speech; for example, from Wikipedia.
3. Read the speech again, more mindful of its context and historic significance.
4. Listen to and watch the speech from the NASA website. http://er.jsc.nasa.gov/seh/ricetalk.htm
5. Read the entire speech again.
6. Select a portion of the speech that you like: A few lines are enough. Write them down in a way that makes reading easy. Stand up. Say these lines out slowly and loudly—as if you are speaking to an audience. Do not

look down while reading and talk at the same time. We will work on this together, later in the chapter.

I ask that you look upon the following speech as a gold standard, a standard that you must aspire to. If you do not believe that you will get there, that's OK. Just read the quotation at the beginning of this chapter again and keep moving forward. Four percent at a time: more of this approach in another chapter.

I think this is one of the most unique speeches in history. I do not think any speech in history has been more endorsed by PM&Es. I do not think that any speech in history fired-up more PM&Es. I wonder if any speech in history did more to ignite young minds to dream of engineering careers. I wonder if this speech should be given even more credit for what subsequently happened in Silicon Valley.

Some background from Wikipedia: *The* "***Address at Rice University on the Nation's Space Effort***," *or better known simply as the* "***We choose to go to the moon***" *speech, was delivered by then U.S.* ***President John F. Kennedy*** *in front of a large crowd gathered at* ***Rice University*** *in Houston, on* ***September 12, 1962.*** *It was one of Kennedy's earlier speeches meant to persuade the American people to support the effort of NASA.*

"We choose to go to the moon" speech (Rice University)
http://er.jsc.nasa.gov/seh/ricetalk.htm

Here we go. Here is President John F. Kennedy at Rice University on September 12, 1962.

We meet at a college noted for knowledge ... in a city noted for progress ... in a State noted for strength ... and we stand in need of all three ... for we meet in an hour of change and challenge ... in a decade of hope and fear ... in an age of both knowledge and ignorance. The greater our knowledge increases

... the greater our ignorance unfolds.

Despite the striking fact that most of the scientists that the world has ever known are alive and working today ... despite the fact that this Nation's own scientific manpower is doubling every 12 years in a rate of growth more than three times that of our population as a whole ... despite that ... the vast stretches of the unknown and the unanswered and the unfinished still far outstrip our collective comprehension.

No man can fully grasp how far and how fast we have come ... but condense ... if you will ... the 50,000 years of man's recorded history in a time span of but a half-century. Stated in these terms ... we know very little about the first 40 years ... except at the end of them advanced man had learned to use the skins of animals to cover them. Then about 10 years ago ... under this standard ... man emerged from his caves to construct other kinds of shelter. Only five years ago man learned to write and use a cart with wheels. Christianity began less than two years ago. The printing press came this year ... and then less than two months ago ... during this whole 50-year span of human history ... the steam engine provided a new source of power.

Newton explored the meaning of gravity. Last month electric lights and telephones and automobiles and airplanes became available. Only last week did we develop penicillin and television and nuclear power ... and now if America's new spacecraft succeeds in reaching Venus ... we will have literally reached the stars before midnight tonight.

This is a breathtaking pace ... and such a pace cannot help but create new ills as it dispels old ... new ignorance ... new problems ... new dangers. Surely the opening vistas of space promise high costs and hardships ... as well as high reward.

So it is not surprising that some would have us stay where we are a little longer to rest ... to wait. But this city of Houston

... this State of Texas ... this country of the United States was not built by those who waited and rested and wished to look behind them. This country was conquered by those who moved forward ... and so will space.

William Bradford ... speaking in 1630 of the founding of the Plymouth Bay Colony ... said that all great and honorable actions are accompanied with great difficulties ... and both must be enterprised and overcome with answerable courage.

If this capsule history of our progress teaches us anything ... it is that man ... in his quest for knowledge and progress ... is determined and cannot be deterred. The exploration of space will go ahead ... whether we join in it or not ... and it is one of the great adventures of all time ... and no nation which expects to be the leader of other nations can expect to stay behind in the race for space.

Those who came before us made certain that this country rode the first waves of the industrial revolutions ... the first waves of modern invention ... and the first wave of nuclear power ... and this generation does not intend to founder in the backwash of the coming age of space. We mean to be a part of it--we mean to lead it. For the eyes of the world now look into space ... to the moon and to the planets beyond ... and we have vowed that we shall not see it governed by a hostile flag of conquest ... but by a banner of freedom and peace. We have vowed that we shall not see space filled with weapons of mass destruction ... but with instruments of knowledge and understanding.

Yet the vows of this Nation can only be fulfilled if we in this Nation are first ... and ... therefore ... we intend to be first. In short ... our leadership in science and in industry ... our hopes for peace and security ... our obligations to ourselves as well as others ... all require us to make this effort ... to solve these mysteries ... to solve them for the good of all men ... and to become the world's leading space-faring nation.

We set sail on this new sea because there is new knowledge to be gained ... and new rights to be won ... and they must be won and used for the progress of all people. For space science ... like nuclear science and all technology ... has no conscience of its own. Whether it will become a force for good or ill depends on man ... and only if the United States occupies a position of pre-eminence can we help decide whether this new ocean will be a sea of peace or a new terrifying theater of war. I do not say the we should or will go unprotected against the hostile misuse of space any more than we go unprotected against the hostile use of land or sea ... but I do say that space can be explored and mastered without feeding the fires of war ... without repeating the mistakes that man has made in extending his writ around this globe of ours.

There is no strife ... no prejudice ... no national conflict in outer space as yet. Its hazards are hostile to us all. Its conquest deserves the best of all mankind ... and its opportunity for peaceful cooperation many never come again. But why ... some say ... the moon? Why choose this as our goal? And they may well ask why climb the highest mountain? Why ... 35 years ago ... fly the Atlantic? Why does Rice play Texas?

We choose to go to the moon. We choose to go to the moon in this decade and do the other things ... not because they are easy ... but because they are hard ... because that goal will serve to organize and measure the best of our energies and skills ... because that challenge is one that we are willing to accept ... one we are unwilling to postpone ... and one which we intend to win ... and the others ... too.

It is for these reasons that I regard the decision last year to shift our efforts in space from low to high gear as among the most important decisions that will be made during my incumbency in the office of the Presidency.

In the last 24 hours we have seen facilities now being created for the greatest and most complex exploration in man's history. We have felt the ground shake and the air shattered by the testing of a Saturn C-1 booster rocket ... many times as powerful as the Atlas which launched John Glenn ... generating power equivalent to 10, 000 automobiles with their accelerators on the floor. We have seen the site where the F-1 rocket engines ... each one as powerful as all eight engines of the Saturn combined ... will be clustered together to make the advanced Saturn missile ... assembled in a new building to be built at Cape Canaveral as tall as a 48 story structure ... as wide as a city block ... and as long as two lengths of this field.

Within these last 19 months at least 45 satellites have circled the earth. Some 40 of them were "made in the United States of America" and they were far more sophisticated and supplied far more knowledge to the people of the world than those of the Soviet Union.

The Mariner spacecraft now on its way to Venus is the most intricate instrument in the history of space science. The accuracy of that shot is comparable to firing a missile from Cape Canaveral and dropping it in this stadium between the 40-yard lines.

Transit satellites are helping our ships at sea to steer a safer course. Tiros satellites have given us unprecedented warnings of hurricanes and storms ... and will do the same for forest fires and icebergs.

We have had our failures ... but so have others ... even if they do not admit them. And they may be less public.

To be sure ... we are behind ... and will be behind for some time in manned flight. But we do not intend to stay behind ... and in this decade ... we shall make up and move ahead.

The growth of our science and education will be enriched by new knowledge of our universe and environment ... by new techniques of learning and mapping and observation ... by new tools and computers for industry ... medicine ... the home as well as the school. Technical institutions ... such as Rice ... will reap the harvest of these gains.

And finally ... the space effort itself ... while still in its infancy ... has already created a great number of new companies ... and tens of thousands of new jobs. Space and related industries are generating new demands in investment and skilled personnel ... and this city and this State ... and this region ... will share greatly in this growth. What was once the furthest outpost on the old frontier of the West will be the furthest outpost on the new frontier of science and space. Houston ... your City of Houston ... with its Manned Spacecraft Center ... will become the heart of a large scientific and engineering community. During the next 5 years the National Aeronautics and Space Administration expects to double the number of scientists and engineers in this area ... to increase its outlays for salaries and expenses to US $60 million a year; to invest some US $200 million in plant and laboratory facilities; and to direct or contract for new space efforts over US $1 billion from this Center in this City.

To be sure ... all this costs us all a good deal of money. This year's space budget is three times what it was in January 1961 ... and it is greater than the space budget of the previous eight years combined. That budget now stands at US $5,400 million a year—a staggering sum ... though somewhat less than we pay for cigarettes and cigars every year. Space expenditures will soon rise some more ... from 40 cents per person per week to more than 50 cents a week for every man ... woman and child in the United States ... for we have given this program a high national priority--even though I realize that this is in some measure an act of faith and vision ... for we do not now know what benefits await us.

But if I were to say ... my fellow citizens ... that we shall send to the moon ... 240,000 miles away from the control station in Houston ... a giant rocket more than 300 feet tall ... the length of this football field ... made of new metal alloys ... some of which have not yet been invented ... capable of standing heat and stresses several times more than have ever been experienced ... fitted together with a precision better than the finest watch ... carrying all the equipment needed for propulsion ... guidance ... control ... communications ... food and survival ... on an untried mission ... to an unknown celestial body ... and then return it safely to earth ... re-entering the atmosphere at speeds of over 25,000 miles per hour ... causing heat about half that of the temperature of the sun--almost as hot as it is here today--and do all this ... and do it right ... and do it first before this decade is out--then we must be bold.

I'm the one who is doing all the work ... so we just want you to stay cool for a minute. [laughter]

However ... I think we're going to do it ... and I think that we must pay what needs to be paid. I don't think we ought to waste any money ... but I think we ought to do the job. And this will be done in the decade of the sixties. It may be done while some of you are still here at school at this college and university. It will be done during the term of office of some of the people who sit here on this platform. But it will be done. And it will be done before the end of this decade.

I am delighted that this university is playing a part in putting a man on the moon as part of a great national effort of the United States of America.

Many years ago the great British explorer George Mallory ... who was to die on Mount Everest ... was asked why did he want to climb it. He said ... "Because it is there."

Well ... space is there ... and we're going to climb it ... and the moon and the planets are there ... and new hopes for knowledge and peace are there. And ... therefore ... as we set sail we ask

God's blessing on the most hazardous and dangerous and greatest adventure on which man has ever embarked.

This speech still takes my breath away!

Trivia: According to the PBS documentary (American Experience series) "Silicon Valley," by the mid-1960s NASA was buying 60% of Integrated Circuits produced in the US and driving growth of seminal companies like Fairchild. Fairchild become something like a seedpod that just scattered new companies all over the valley; and that's what really started what we call the modern Silicon Valley.

After you have finished steps 1 to 5, (initial read, background and context update, read again, watch and listen, read again) let us continue to step 6. Take all the necessary time with step 6. Seldom will the benefit to effort ratio be higher for you in your public speaking voyage.

Select a portion of the speech that you like: a few lines are enough. I have selected these lines from the Wikipedia article: *Its hazards are hostile to us all. Its conquest deserves the best of all mankind, and its opportunity for peaceful cooperation may never come again. But why, some say, the moon? Why choose this as our goal? And they may well ask why climb the highest mountain? Why, 35 years ago, fly the Atlantic? Why does Rice play Texas? We choose to go to the moon. We choose to go to the moon in this decade and do the other things, not because they are easy, but because they are hard, because that goal will serve to organize and measure the best of our energies and skills, because that challenge is one that we are willing to accept, one we are unwilling to postpone, and one which we intend to win, and the others, too.*

I came across a very good public speaking technique in a book called *Speak Like Churchill, Stand Like Lincoln: 21 Powerful Secrets of History's Greatest Speakers* by James C Hume. I truly wish I had come across this technique at the very start of my public speaking voyage, and not have had to wait four to five years for this gem. Frankly I am puzzled that I never came across it before, or why it is absent from the other books and products I have.

I recommend that you plan on purchasing this book and plan on eventually reading it syntopically with *Necessary Bridges*. Chapter 12 is called "Power Reading." Here is the technique summarized.

Never, never, never let words come out of your mouth when your eyes are looking down.

You must be looking at your audience when you are speaking.

Hume calls it both the *See-Stop-Say technique* and the *Churchill/Roosevelt/Reagan method.*

Here is the technique broken down into steps:

1. Look down at the line you're about to read out and take an imaginary "snapshot" of the words you see.
2. Bring your head up.
3. Pause.
4. Looking at an audience member (or an object in your room if you are practicing alone) "conversationalize" what you have just memorized. Say it to the audience member as you would if speaking to only one person.
5. Look down again and "snapshot" the next chunk of words.
6. Look up.
7. Pause.
8. Look at another audience member and conversationalize. and so on.

You may feel awkward, stupid, embarrassed, but public speaking is never about you: It is about the audience, and this way they are absorbing what you are saying. The pause gives listeners time to digest what you have just said. And in case you didn't yet know, the pause is the most powerful tool in all of speaking. Pauses are what make a speech sound conversational. While a speech is most certainly not a conversation, it must nonetheless sound and seem conversational. Hume sums it up this way. *The pause may feel and seem awkward or jarring to you, but to your audience you'll be sounding like Winston Churchill, Franklin Roosevelt, or Ronald Reagan.*

An interesting observation—Hume points out that this is more of an eye-hand skill than a mental one. People who are good at sports pick up this the easiest. And just like sports, this has to be practiced a lot to acquire expertise.

Now it's your turn to read out the lines you have selected from the speech. Before starting you will have to modify your notes to this format. This is EXERCISE #4.

READ & MEMORIZE—TAKE A MENTAL SNAPSHOT
Its hazards are hostile to us all.
LOOK UP AT AN AUDIENCE MEMBER
PAUSE
SAY IT CONVERSATIONALLY—ALOUD
Its hazards are hostile to us all.
LOOK DOWN ONLY AFTER YOU HAVE FINISHED
SPEAKING
READ AND MEMORIZE
Its conquest deserves the best of all mankind
PAUSE
and its opportunity for peaceful cooperation may never come again
PAUSE
But why, some say, the moon? Why choose this as our goal?
PAUSE
And they may well ask why climb the highest mountain? ...

AND SO ON
Why, 35 years ago, fly the Atlantic? ...
Why does Rice play Texas? ...
We choose to go to the moon ...
We choose to go to the moon in this decade ...
and do the other things ...
not because they are easy, but because they are hard ...
because that goal ...
will serve to organize and measure the best of our energies and skills ...
because that challenge is one that we are willing to accept ...
one we are unwilling to postpone ...
and one which we intend to win ...
and the others, too.

If you have gone through this chapter sincerely, and spoken out loud, using the Churchill/Roosevelt/Reagan method, you have taken your first necessary steps toward PS&ST expertise. More importantly you have got a taste, a strong sense of what public speaking is about. If you felt strong sensations, feelings, anxieties, embarrassments—in your body—while going through this, welcome to the world of public speaking. It happens to all of us. We are not that different.

Trivia: if you should ever visit Space Center Houston, you can see, and perhaps even stand behind, the very podium that President John F. Kennedy used for this speech.

Final note on this speech, again from Wikipedia: *Douglas Brinkley, a professor of history at Rice University, wrote in looking back on the speech on its 50th anniversary that: Kennedy's oration was front-page news around the country. Pundits saw it as another Ted Sorenson-penned speech drenched in terrestrial aspiration. But **for all of its soaring*** *rhetoric, the Rice address was* **grounded in pragmatism**. *Kennedy made the case to taxpayers that NASA needed a US $5.4 billion budget. Kennedy also did a tremendous job of connecting the moonshot to Houston in ways that thrilled locals. "We meet at a college noted for knowledge, in a city noted for progress, in a state noted for strength," he said. "And we stand in need of all three."* **What Kennedy did so brilliantly that day was frame the moonshot as being instrumental for U.S. security reasons.**

Someday fellow engineer, fellow project manager, you may well have to make a case for more money for your project, or for your team, or for expanding your ventures, or even for security reasons. If you can masterfully combine soaring rhetoric and grounded pragmatism this way, and make your case; then your boss does not stand a chance, even if he or she does not have the funds.

... and do all this ... and do it right ... and do it first ... we must be bold!

Here's my *fifth wish* for you, "When it comes your time to masterfully combine soaring rhetoric with pragmatism: may you always do it right, and most of all, may you always be bold!"

That reminds me of a story of negotiation from my own home. My wife routinely out-negotiates me with pretend meekness. I even wrote a humorous speech on this. Its title— what else? "Out-Negotiated." Once, decades ago, when our son was very young, she asked out loud to no one in particular, if she could buy something. Our tiny-tot son's counsel, "Mum, if you want a dog from Dad ... ask for a horse!" That boy's going to be an awesome negotiator!

Dear PM&Es, when you need to raise funds for your ventures from your bosses or investors, PS&ST expertise can be your great lever.

As I have been writing *Necessary Bridges*, my wife Anahita, an outstanding Toastmaster, has been reviewing it. Her comment: "Way too much testosterone in this chapter. What about the women engineers and women project managers? They may not tune into this 'Moon' speech the way you guys do. Give them another speaking exercise." Obediently, I shall comply.

Please go through steps 1–5 with Hillary Rodham Clinton's Remarks to the U.N. 4th World Conference on Women Plenary Session on September 5, 1995, in Beijing, China. Then practice speaking out loud with this segment—as in step 6. The Churchill/Roosevelt/Reagan method—remember? This is EXERCISE #5.

http://www.americanrhetoric.com/speeches/hillary-clintonbeijingspeech.htm

These abuses have continued because ... for too long ... the history of women has been a history of silence. Even today ... there are those who are trying to silence our words.

But the voices of this conference and of the women at Huairou must be heard loudly and clearly ...

It is a violation of human rights when babies are denied food ... or drowned ... or suffocated ... or their spines broken ... simply because they are born girls.

It is a violation of human rights when women and girls are sold into the slavery of prostitution ... for human greed ... and the kinds of reasons that are used to justify this practice should no longer be tolerated.

It is a violation of human rights when women are doused with gasoline ... set on fire ... and burned to death because their marriage dowries are deemed too small.

It is a violation of human rights when individual women are raped in their own communities ... and when thousands of women are subjected to rape as a tactic or prize of war.

It is a violation of human rights when a leading cause of death worldwide among women ages 14 to 44 ... is the violence they are subjected to in their own homes by their own relatives.

It is a violation of human rights when young girls are brutalized ... by the painful and degrading practice of genital mutilation.

It is a violation of human rights when women are denied the right to plan their own families ... and that includes being forced to have abortions ... or being sterilized against their will.

If there is one message that echoes forth from this conference ... let it be that human rights are women's rights ... and women's rights are human rights ... once and for all.

Trivia: American Rhetoric: Top 100 Speeches, ranks this talk at #35.

For a contemporary commentary on gender differences, check out Daniel Goleman's book *The Brain and Emotional Intelligence: New Insights.* One conclusion is: *The analysis reveals that while in general you find gender differences among the various competencies, when you only look at the pool of star performers (people in the top ten percent of business performance) those differences wash out. The men are as good as the women, the women as good as the men, across the board.*

This is another validation of the argument that PS&ST expertise will enable your upward-professional-mobility. A serendipitous and bonus benefit of expertise in PS&ST is the increase of EI. To put it bluntly, to be successful at PS&ST you must know what you and your audiences are feeling—at all times. It's what really matters—only those lacking in EI will argue otherwise. We engineers will undoubtedly argue a lot!

If you're a stubborn engineer who makes and constantly wins this "feelings don't count" argument, I predict you may, later on, get left further behind—and while I hope this never, ever happens, you may, without figuring out how, end up amongst the ranks of the CBT (cynical, bitter, and twisted). How are you feeling right now? Offended? Outraged? It counts: Doesn't it? Your feelings count. Period. I respect you too much to pretend otherwise. I want the best for you (and for our professions) too much to pretend otherwise. I hope a day comes when every single CEO has an engineering background. If it doesn't, it's our own fault.

In light of this, it is a good idea to practice both these speech segments **aloud**, preferably standing up, using the Churchill/Roosevelt/Reagan method, regardless of your gender. Don't diminish or restrict your PS&ST aspirations along gender lines. Don't "not-pay-attention" to your own feelings.

If you are now—or envision yourself ever being a high-up executive—this reading technique (Churchill/Roosevelt/Reagan method) could be your distinguishing competency, perhaps even a career saver. But you must start practicing like an athlete—starting now. Increasingly, the higher up you go, you will have to stick to a script. If lawyers are involved, you will likely be "hard-constrained" by a script.

If you read and speak while looking down at your notes, you've lost your audience and you probably do not even know it. Or worse, you do not care too much that you have. That's terrible. You've got to connect and conversationalize. Period.

Well Ms./Mr. Wannabe Big Shot Executive, I admire and respect your aspirations. And Ms./Mr. PM&E who may not care for this kind of over-ambitious thinking, I admire and respect your authentic choices, whatever you wish for, and hope very hard that one of them is to commit to becoming an expert PS&ST, and eventually its evangelizer.

The objective of this chapter has been to get you to aspire to greatness in PS&ST, to set a scorching, high standard for yourself for the voyage ahead.

Don't underestimate the vision thing in the pursuit of

excellence. Do not place practicality and action on a higher (or lower) pedestal than vision thing. Visualizing where you want to be is an equal partner in the process that leads to expertise

I hope this has been achieved. I hope you have your sights on the moon ... and on the stars beyond. I hope you are reaching for a world, where once and for all, human rights are women's rights and women's rights are human rights. Don't think dog, think horse; don't think million, think billion!

If you can figure out ways to fall in love with PS&ST simultaneously—more power to you!

And from Michelangelo to all of us: Beware of the greater danger!

Let me close this lofty "vision thing" chapter with a question from Marianne Williamson, "Who are you not to shine?" Seriously. Please answer the question. "Who are you not to shine?"

"Our deepest fear is not that we are inadequate. Our deepest fear is that we are powerful beyond measure. It is our light, not our darkness that most frightens us. We ask ourselves, "Who am I to be brilliant, gorgeous, talented, and fabulous?" Actually, who are you not to be? Your playing small does not serve the world. There is nothing enlightened about shrinking so that other people will not feel insecure around you. We are all meant to shine, as children do. It is not just in some of us; it is in everyone and as we let our own light shine, we unconsciously give others permission to do the same. As we are liberated from our own fear, our presence automatically liberates others." — *Marianne Williamson*

Chapter 5

Basic Parts of a Speech

"Know your speech craft, and know yourself, and in a hundred presentations you will never be in peril."
— Adaptation of Sun Tzu's acumen

I have stated earlier that in my opinion, PM&Es will find the body of knowledge of PS&ST very easy to intellectually absorb and remember. A timely reminder is due: Learning this body of knowledge is only one part of the training. Putting this book—knowledge—into practice effectively is very different.

This chapter will provide a model of how I will work through the content: the body of knowledge of PS&ST.
- Discuss the basic content
- Provide exercises
- Provides examples
- Suggest external resources to go into more detail

After having studied many books and audio and video products on speech craft, I still assert that working through the Competent Communication manual of Toastmasters International is the best way to learn the basics of public speaking.

At the risk of repeating myself ad-nauseam, one of the best decisions you can make on your voyage to more skillful leadership and communication is to join a Toastmasters club. Here both theoretical knowledge and practice proficiency can be acquired in a respectful, friendly, self-paced, and supportive environment—at great economies. In my city, Houston, Texas, there are almost 200 clubs, and I understand that English is a second language for almost a third of the city's membership. My clubs are very diverse and very inclusive places. Earlier the majority of membership was middle-aged and older, but I am seeing a lot of youngsters joining in now, even younger PM&Es. By and large, my Toastmasters experience has been blind to race, gender, religion, professional background, and income.

If you are a leader in your company, or a team leader at your work place, and you sense that all those around you would benefit from enhanced communication, consider starting a club in your organization. Treat it as a leadership challenge for yourself.

When I started a club in my company, I treated it like a pet project and made my own project charter, project plan, stakeholder management plan, and communication plan. I have no doubt that this made a significant difference. I further treated it as a High Performance Leadership project—which is a part of the Toastmasters International education program, so I had a good structure and guidelines to follow.

That being said, my experience has been that individuals grow significantly quicker in community clubs (which are open to all), than they do in corporate clubs (where membership may be restricted to company employees). Members in community clubs are more engaged. They are participating because they really want to be there: They have made the necessary commitments—time and money. They are generally pursuing stretch goals. In corporate clubs I have sometimes observed more compliance than engagement. Some of the members would prefer to be elsewhere. Commitment of all the members is not a given. Attendance is erratic.

Corporate clubs have some unique challenges relating to the complex and complicated nature of departmental and individual relationships at work. Add to this mix, elements of organizational politics and status-related issues with vertical relationships, and the efficacy of the club can become suboptimal. Corporate club meetings are usually on a very tight one-hour schedule, which poses further issues. I have found that frequently the best feedback occurs unofficially after the meetings. This is an advantage less available to corporate clubs. On the other hand, a corporate club could serve as a truly effective site to bring departments together, to identify and grow future leaders, and to serve as team building enablers. Corporate clubs generally have better access to resources and have better meeting facilities.

So, join a Toastmasters club and you are absolutely on your way to getting a firm grip on the basics of public speaking.

The Toastmasters International Competent Communication manual has 10 speech projects. The first project is called the Ice Breaker. The next three projects are foundational projects, where basic structure and purpose of the speech are identified and illuminated. The next four projects are individual aspects of speaking and speech preparation, like body language, gestures, vocal variety, research, and visual aids. The last two projects bring all the education from the earlier eight projects together, requiring the speaker to persuade powerfully and to inspire audiences.

Doing these ten projects thoroughly, sincerely, and systematically, with the support of a club-assigned mentor, will result in the most rapid phase of growth in your pubic speaking voyage. After this it will be tougher and slower. Refer to the asymptote nature of the acquisition of expertise in chapter 6.

Every speech should have an opening, a body, and a closing. While this is obvious, especially when sitting in comfort and reading a book, it is not always effectively put into practice in the rough and tumble of daily life. When I took some of my early work-related presentations and looked for clear openings, points, transitions, and closings, I was surprised and disappointed with my findings.

Here's an EXERCISE for you: EXERCISE #6. Take one of your (or someone else's) recent presentations and just scribble these words somewhere in the speech or in the margins. Do not worry too much about the exact meaning or technical accuracy of the words. Just use your best intuition and judgment and go for it. If you do not have any idea what the word stands for, no problem; just ignore it. Even if you do not have a written version of the speech, and are using slides to speak, you can still complete the exercise. Here are the words—you must enter most of them somewhere in the speech and then grade your speech for structure and completeness.

1. Strong opening (or weak opening)
2. Transition 1 + signpost / road map (what the speech is about)
3. Point #1
4. Transition 2 (may include a one line summary of point 1)
5. Point #2
6. Transition 3 (may include one line summaries of points 1 & 2)
7. Point #3 (continue with as many transitions and points as necessary)
8. Transition to close (may include a summary of earlier points)
9. Strong close (or weak close)

Additionally if you can insert these words into the margins of the speech it will be helpful:

— Punch line / sound bite / point of wisdom / summary phrase /
— Open-ended question
— Jaw dropping moment/Stunning moment/Magic moment
— Rhetorical device
— Carry out message

— Call to action
— Most memorable / impactful part
— Least effective part
— This is a story.
— This is the point of the story.
— Within a story: this is the conflict: this is the resolution and cure

Some more questions to ask while analyzing the speech:
— In one sentence—what was the purpose of the speech?
— Mission accomplished?
— Mismatch between audience and speaker expectations?
— Mismatch between audience and speaker needs?
— Too complex?
— What did the audience remember? (Ask them—get real world feedback.)
— Wandering aimlessly? Meandering all over the place? (Verbally and physically.)
— Too much information? Too many points? (One of the most basic mistakes.)
— Speech rate (words per minute). Finished in time?
— Too preachy?
— Too much pride / arrogance / superiority / self-promotion?
— Was the speech audience-focused?
— Was the speech boring?
— Was the speech memorable?
— Was it worth the audience's time? Really?

If you feel this exercise was useful, do it with a few more of your past presentations, and then make a list of the mistakes you will never make again.

Another version of this exercise would be to try it with

a famous speech. To do this effectively, you must be very familiar with the speech. Do the exercise only after watching it or listening to it multiple times, and reading the transcript. Put on your ultra-analytical hat and get to work.

For an example of this, consider the Steve Jobs Stanford commencement address. This speech has attained stratospheric status. Here is some background from Walter Isaacson's book, *Steve Jobs*.

Although he rarely gave speeches, outside product demonstrations, he accepted Stanford's invitation to give the June 2005 commencement address. One night he sat down and wrote the speech himself, with no help other than bouncing ideas off his wife. It turned out to be a very intimate and simple talk.

At this point I recommend you watch and enjoy the speech. Next, read the transcript. Finally listen again, but with your "analytical-student" hat on.

Steve Jobs: How to live before you die
http://www.ted.com/talks/steve_jobs_how_to_live_before_you_die

Here are different analyses of the speech.
Steve Jobs Stanford Commencement Address 2005
Analysis: Eleonora Pinto
http://prezi.com/4cafnh0joxk4/steve-jobs-stanford-commencement-address-2005-analysis/
Mind Map of Steve Jobs Stanford Commencement Address: Nathan Chitty
https://www.youtube.com/watch?v=Ul4eI0bQccQ

I have a feeling most PM&Es will enjoy the analyzing of a great speech—much more than the general population, and will make many more efforts to go deep. More power to you!

Here is how Walter Isaacson summarizes the talk.

The artful minimalism of the speech gave it simplicity, purity and charm. Search where you will, from anthologies to YouTube, and you won't find a better commencement address. Others may have been more important ... but none has had more grace.

What is your analysis of the speech? Are you enjoying the process of understanding the basics of a speech? Is there a lot more to it that initially anticipated? Will you continue to be both an analyst and practitioner of PS&ST?

Why don't you try to analyze your earlier presentations using the Eleonora Pinto and Nathan Chitty models. It's all a learning experience.

Here is my *sixth wish* for you: May you someday give at least one unforgettable, artful, and minimal talk; with the simplicity, purity, charm, and grace of the Stanford June 2005 commencement. Even if it is no more than a one-on-one within a family, or to a small group of volunteers, or to your team at work, you can do it.

I hope you have a newfound appreciation of how a speech is structured. And perhaps you will consider more seriously the need to evangelize PS&ST to PM&Es—especially students and younger professionals.

Here is a list of the Toastmasters Competent Communication manual projects with objectives of each speech project in question format. Consider using this as a checklist when preparing your future speeches.

Project 1: Icebreaker
Ready to start? Ready to discover current skills and weaknesses? Ready to share yourself?

Foundational Skills
Project 2: Organize Your Speech
Opening strong? Message clear? Transitions clear? Closing strong? Outline appropriate?
Project 3: Get to the Point
General purpose (inform, educate, entertain, persuade, inspire) and specific purpose identified?
Project 4: How to Say It
Correct words and sentences in place? Rhetorical devises included? Jargon eliminated?

Specific Skills
Project 5: Your Body Speaks
Thought about movement, gestures, expressions, and eye contact?
Project 6: Vocal Variety
Thought about when to speed up and slow down? Planned when to speak loudly and softly? Decided where to pause?
Project 7: Research Your Topic
PM&Es are very good at this. Do not over-research.
Project 8: Visual Aids
More than just a projector and slides?

Bringing it all together
Project 9: Persuade with Power
Will this message really persuade my audience?
Project 10: Inspire Your Audience
Will this message really inspire my audience?

If you have a significant number of "yes" answers, you have got the basics of the speech in place. If not, negotiate harder with yourself to work harder. Keep repeating until you are satisfied. The process will take time and can feel overwhelming.

Setting realistic learning and progress targets is the solution.

There are many different speech structure models and many advance structures. I will consider those beyond the scope of this book. I will point you to resources to develop more advanced speeches. As you have a project plan and you have committed time and budget, here are some items that you may wish to consider procuring. These are for getting alternate perspectives and details on the basics parts of a speech.

Harvard Business Review
"How to Give a Killer Presentation: Lessons from TED" by Chris Anderson
June 2013 REPRINT R1306K

Chris Anderson is the TED curator and the entrepreneur I most associate with TED Talks, which are usually short, powerful talks. TED is where a lot of the hottest action is occurring in the world of public speaking. Anderson's, HBR article is an excellent summary of basics, best practices, and most common mistakes associated with public speaking and presentations. It is a quick and essential read, perhaps 15–20 minutes. (Price in August November 2014 from HBR website = US $8.95)

12 Ways to Become a Speaking Star: What Hollywood Can Teach You about Great Presentation Skills by Patricia Fripp

Patricia Fripp is a legend in the public speaking world. She was the first female president of the National Speakers Association and, on my list, is a trailblazer. She is a speech coach to top executives, etc.; the list of her accomplishments is long. This is a short e-book. Allow around 30 minutes to complete reading the book. (Price in August 2014 from Amazon website = US $2.99 Kindle Edition) Disclosure: I am a current student of her online training course FrippVT.

If you have joined Toastmasters, and/or gone though some of your past presentations and inserted the words as instructed, and/or analyzed a famous speech and inserted the words as instructed, and/or gone through the Eleonora Pinto and Nathan Chitty review of the 2005 Stanford commencement structure, and /or reviewed one of your presentations against the checklist questions from the CC 10 projects, and/or gone through the recommended HBR TED article and Fripp book, then you should be conversant with the basic parts of a speech.

If not, turn to your sponsor and your support partner for help. This is no time to get stuck. We've just started. Do not forget: You are an ambassador for your profession at all times—whether you know it or not; whether you acknowledge it or not; whether you like it or not.

Don't get sloppy: Don't falter on your commitment. *We are all caught in an inescapable network of mutuality. Whatever affects one directly, affects all indirectly.* Do your bit.

A few days ago, I got this update from Ash.

Icebreaker completed. Club mentor in place. Preparing speech 2: will be delivered in 3 weeks. Have signed up for the Toastmaster role. My club mentor encouraged me to do this and will guide me; feeling anxious, but will give it all I got. Got the HBR article and read it—excellent! Got the Fripp e-book and completed it—full of simple and creative insights: very useful. Have not yet analyzed my earlier speeches (as set out in this chapter) but listened to the Stanford commencement and went through the YouTube analysis. Awesome speech—thanks for pointing me to this one. Mom & Dad loved it too.

Thanks. ... Ash

This next message is not fictional. It is an actual message I received from an engineer (with English as a second language) who recently joined one of my clubs, and requested that I be his mentor. It is reproduced with his permission.

Rashid,

I would like to thank you for the great advice and for encouraging and inspiring me for my first speech yesterday. I received a lot of great notes that make me more and more encouraged to go on and work hard toward my future speeches and to develop my communication skills. It felt really good reading all those notes and hearing those words from people who are great speakers. I have started working on my next project and I will be more confident this time because of all the support and encouragement from you and other members of the club.

Thank you again.

Jay

Dear Reader, have you committed and started PS&ST yet? If yes—excellent! If no—as soon as you do, good things will follow.

Chapter 6

The Fittest Speaker: The Expert Speaker

"Physical fitness is not only one of the most important keys to a healthy body; it is the basis of dynamic and creative intellectual activity."
— *John F. Kennedy*

This chapter does not directly relate to PS&ST, however, I feel these ideas — reminders mostly — could have a hugely beneficial effect for anyone seeking expertise in any field. Indeed, I will not be too surprised if some readers conclude that this chapter is the most beneficial of the entire book.

I am including this chapter in *Necessary Bridges* because one of my commitments to you is to share what I have learned on my PS&ST voyage. Deliberate and planned rest combined with deliberate and planned exercise made such an astonishing difference to my mental pre-speech state, stage energy and presence, that I would be remiss not to share, indeed persuasively advocate, this finding with and to you. I would feel almost like I am withholding a critical finding from you. So rather than do that, I will leave you with this: Reading this chapter is optional. If you already have excellent and healthy habits, please feel free to proceed to the next chapter.

I try and put what follows into daily practice, with discipline, determination, and devotion. I am convinced that I am a significantly better PS&ST for it. I am convinced that if you do the same, you will at least come to be recognized as "The Fittest Speaker," and this is no small advantage.

Back to the movie *Invictus* and another scene that has long stuck with me. The South African rugby team, after a string of poor international performances, has new management and has just been put through a very rigorous workout. The assistant coach says to the head coach, *"I reckon you've knocked the stuffing out of them today."* The head coach responds with, *"I haven't even begun. We may not be the most* *talented team in the world … **but we're sure as hell going to be the fittest.***"

Later in the movie, toward the end of the championship game, the payoff is clear. At the end of regulation time, for the first time in Rugby World Cup history, the score (of the final match) is tied. As the South African team walks back onto the field in extra time, the captain repeatedly asks and reminds his teammates, *"Who's the fittest team on the field? Who's the fittest team on the field?"* Fitness proves to be a deciding advantage. The South African team goes on to win the World Cup in overtime.

This thing called fitness may be one of the greatest gifts, greatest advantages, we can confer on ourselves. Not just physical fitness, but fitness in all domains of life.

As a matter of fact, we can even become more fit in the way we read. I pointed you to *How to Read a Book* in the preface of *Necessary Bridges*. I consider reading that book and picking up all the insights and best practices from that book as improving your general reading fitness. As surely as the head coach of the South African rugby team decided "we may not be the most talented team in the world … *but we're sure as hell going to be the fittest,"* we too can decide, "we may not be the most talented readers in the world, *but we sure as hell can be the fittest."* We can all progress from elementary readers, to inspectional readers, to analytical readers to syntopical readers the same way the South African rugby team worked on improving its fitness.

Let's start with physical fitness. I am predicting that if you do nothing to improve any of your PS&ST skills, and only improve your physical fitness, you will become a more effective PS&ST anyway. I have been repeatedly surprised at how much PS&ST resembles a sporting activity. Indeed this seems to be one of the best-kept secrets of public speaking.

Two of the best and most economic ways to improve physical fitness are disciplined sleep routines and regular physical exercise routines.

Sleep

Fortunately, an awareness of the advantages of proper sleep seems to be spreading rapidly. Using a syntopical reading approach, start out by viewing these four TED talks, and then read the transcripts.

Arianna Huffington: "How to succeed? Get more sleep."
http://www.ted.com/talks/arianna_huffington_how_to_succeed_get_more_sleep#t-54943
Jessa Gamble: "Our natural sleep cycle"
http://www.ted.com/talks/jessa_gamble_how_to_sleep/transcript?language=en
Russell Foster: "Why do we sleep?"
http://www.ted.com/talks/russell_foster_why_do_we_sleep
Jeff Iliff: "One more reason to get a good night's sleep"
http://www.ted.com/talks/jeff_iliff_one_more_reason_to_get_a_good_night_s_sleep
Next, read this article
Harvard Business Review
"Why We Humblebrag About Being Busy" by Greg McKeown
http://blogs.hbr.org/2014/06/why-we-humblebrag-about-being-busy/

This section of the HBR article really jumped out at me.
Rest Well to Excel: *K Anders Ericsson* (considered by many to be the world's foremost expert on expertise) *found*

*that a significant difference between good performers and excellent performers was the number of hours they spent practicing... What few people realize is that the **second most highly correlated factor distinguishing the good from the great is how much they sleep.** As Ericsson pointed out, top-performing violinists slept more than less accomplished violinists: averaging 8.6 hours of sleep every 24 hours.*

Here are a couple of thought-provoking nuggets about sleep that I picked up from the book *The Willpower Instinct* by Kelly McGonigal, Ph.D.

If you are surviving on less than six hours of sleep a night, there's a good chance you don't even remember what it is like to have your full willpower.

If you are chronically sleep deprived, you may find yourself feeling regret at the end of the day, wondering why you gave in to temptation. It's easy to let this spiral into guilt and shame. **It hardly ever occurs to us that we don't need to become better people, but to become better-rested people.**

The point I want to make with this section is that if we deliberately plan the number of hours we sleep, create healthy pre-sleep routines, and wake up in the morning feeling grateful and energized, we will be better PS&ST (and PM&Es) for this commitment. I cannot prove it, but this has been my experience. It's worth trying out. Good luck!

Exercise

The closest thing to a true wonder drug is exercise. While we are all fully aware of this, we nonetheless find ourselves committing suboptimally to regular exercise.

In her book *The Willpower Instinct*, author Kelly McGonigal reports on the conclusion of a study (Megan Oaten and Ken

Cheng, Macquarie University, Sydney Australia) where the researchers were stunned by their findings. They had hoped for positive results, but were pleasantly surprised by how far-reaching the treatment's effects were. After two months of this treatment, the benefits included (1) improvement in attention, (2) increased ability to ignore distractions, (3) reduced smoking, drinking, and caffeine intake, (4) eating less junk food, (4) spending less time on TV, (4) spending more times studying, (5) saving more money by spending less on impulse purchases and (6) less procrastination. The author writes: *Good God what is this miracle drug and where can I get a prescription? The intervention wasn't a drug at all. The willpower miracle was physical exercise. The participants, none of whom exercised regularly before the intervention, were given free membership to a gym and encouraged to make good use of it ... The researchers asked them not to make any other changes in their lives ... Exercise turns out to be the closest thing to a wonder drug that self-control scientists have discovered. The willpower benefits are immediate ... The long term effects are even more impressive ... Physical exercise (like meditation) makes your brain bigger and faster, and the prefrontal cortex shows the largest training effect.*

And on and on it goes. I can say that I have experienced nothing but benefits after committing to run regularly.

An interesting nugget that I picked up from the same book is this: As far as willpower and self-control go, it may be better to exercise for five minutes every hour, instead of one equivalent longer session daily. I have experimented with this too—and I think it helps. I still do my daily run, but when I squeeze in some combination of breathing and vigorous body movements for three to five minutes every hour, I am in a better mood, more energized, a quicker learner and probably more productive. So at least give it a try: with discipline, determination, and devotion.

Here are some of my highlights from the book *What I Talk About, When I Talk About Running* by world-famous author Haruki Murakami. I have been greatly inspired by his stories and example: I hope it inspires you too. Remember the *Invictus* scene from the preface? How do we exceed our own expectations? How do we get better than we think we can be? How do we inspire ourselves to greatness, when nothing else will do? How do we inspire everyone around us? By using the work of others! Well Haruki Murakami is one of the "others" who has greatly inspired me. From his book:

I started running in the fall of 1982 and have been running since then for nearly twenty-three years. Over this period, I've jogged almost every day, run in at least one marathon every year.

Along with this, my diet started to gradually change as well. I began to eat mostly vegetables, with fish as my main source of protein.

Running every day is a kind of lifeline for me, so I'm not going to lay off or quit just because I'm busy. If I used being busy as an excuse not to run, I'd never run again. **I have only a few reasons to keep on running, and a truckload of them to quit.** *All I can do is keep those few reasons nicely polished.*

And finally this highlight—it truly astonished me!

My pulse is generally about fifty beats per minute, which I think is pretty slow. (By the way I've heard that the gold medalist at the Sydney Olympics Naoko Takahashi, has a pulse of thirty-five.) But if I run for about thirty minutes it rises to seventy. After I run as hard as I can, it gets near one hundred.

Here are a couple of running-related TED Talks that I turn to, to keep my motivation high:

Christopher McDougall: "Are we born to run?"

http://www.ted.com/talks/christopher_mcdougall_are_
we_born_to_run
May El-Khalil: "Making peace is a marathon"
http://www.ted.com/talks/may_el_khalil_making_peace_
is_a_marathon

Hope you enjoy them and draw inspiration from them: but also study the speeches to see what the speakers did well as speakers. Print out the transcript and do the "basics of a speech" exercise on one of these speeches.

And finally, one more clip that inspired me. Here is a man who starts serious and disciplined running in his 80s and goes on to become an icon to many of us.

101-year-old Fauja Singh Runs the London Marathon—Horizon: Eat, Fast and Live Longer: https://www.youtube.com/watch?v=gCY0Xx92YvQ

A bonus for speakers and presenters who chose to run regularly, is that almost all of them use the running time to work and rework their speeches, to practice, to memorize, to visualize, and to brainstorm what questions the audience may have for them during a question and answer session.

To sum up, it is my contention and my direct experience that a commitment to regular exercise and sensible sleep routines **alone** will make anyone a better PS&ST (or PM&E).

Here is my *seventh wish* for you. I hope you find a coach who convinces you *"you may not be the most talented person in the world ... but you sure as hell can be the fittest."*

I know for myself, that if I plan a deep sleep and a round of exercise prior to any presentation, the speech goes much better. I cannot prove it. I can certainly continue experimenting and tuning—and I will. At the very least, you can do the same. Try it yourself and see if it works for you.

Acquiring Expertise

Our shared goal is to acquire expertise in PS&ST. I recommend that you syntopically read this HBR article. The price is US $8.95, and this may be the best US $8.95 you ever spend. If you have children, consider exposing them to this line of thinking, and the potential payoff could be enormous.

Making of an Expert: by K. Anders Ericsson, Michael J. Prietula, Edward T. Cokely
(Source: Harvard Business Review 9 pages. Publication Date: Jul 01, 2007. Prod. #: R0707J-PDF-ENG)
https://hbr.org/2007/07/the-making-of-an-expert

Summary of the article from the HBR website:
Popular lore tells us that genius is born, not made. Scientific research, on the other hand, reveals that true expertise is mainly the product of years of intense practice and dedicated coaching. Ordinary practice is not enough: To reach elite levels of performance, you need to constantly push yourself beyond your abilities and comfort level. Such discipline is the key to becoming an expert in all domains, including management and leadership. Those are the conclusions reached by Anders Ericsson, a professor of psychology at Florida State University; Michael Prietula, a professor at the Goizueta Business School; and Edward Cokely, a research fellow at the Max Planck Institute for Human Development, who together studied data on the behavior of experts gathered by more than 100 scientists. What consistently distinguished elite surgeons, chess players, writers, athletes, pianists, and other experts was the habit of engaging in "deliberate" practice—a sustained focus on tasks that they couldn't do before. Experts continually analyzed what they did wrong, adjusted their techniques, and worked

arduously to correct their errors. Even such traits as charisma can be developed using this technique. Working with a drama school, the authors created a set of acting exercises for managers that remarkably enhanced executives' powers of charm and persuasion. Through deliberate practice, leaders can improve their ability to win over their employees, their peers, or their board of directors. The journey to elite performance is not for the impatient or the faint of heart. It takes at least a decade and requires the guidance of an expert teacher to provide tough, often painful feedback. It also demands would-be experts to develop their "inner coach" and eventually drive their own progress.

If you feel the article resonated with your thinking, then strongly consider procuring these excellent books. They opened my eyes to an entirely new world. I hope they do the same for you too. These books have my high recommendation.

Bounce: Mozart, Federer, Picasso, Beckham, and the Science of Success by Matthew Syed
Talent is Overrated: What Really Separates World-Class Performers from Everybody Else by Geoff Colvin
Outliers: The Story of Success by Malcolm Gladwell

Here are some more thoughts related to the acquisition of expertise that I have picked up while reading.

This nugget is from *Talent is Overrated:*

Noel Tichy, a professor at the University of Michigan business school and former chief of General Electric's famous Crotonville management development center, uses a diagram of three concentric circles. He labels the inner circle "comfort circle," the middle one the "learning zone," and the outer one "panic zone." Only by choosing activities in the learning zone can one make progress. That's the location of skills and abilities that are just out of reach. We can never make progress in the comfort zone because these are activities we can already do easily, while the panic zone activities are so hard that we don't even know how to approach them. Identifying the learning zone, which is not simple, and then forcing oneself to stay continually in it as it changes, which is even harder—these are the first and most important characteristics of deliberate practice.

And deliberate practice is the sure road to expertise.

Here is a great insight on expertise or mastery. This one is from Daniel Pink's book called *Drive: The Surprising Truth About What Motivates Us.*

Mastery (or the acquisition of expertise) *is an asymptote.*

An asymptote (in this case a horizontal asymptote) is a straight line that a curve approaches but never quite reaches.

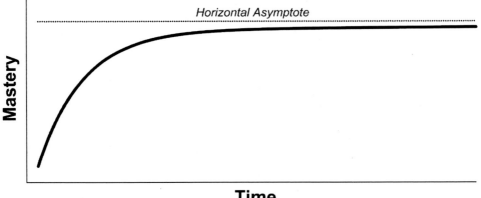

Acquisition of expertise is most rapid initially. Then it takes more and more time, and more and more effort, to make less and less progress. Understanding this prevents us from erroneously concluding that we have plateaued and it is no use to practice further. The error lies in believing that progress toward mastery is linear.

You can approach mastery, you can get really, really close to it, but you can never touch it. Mastery is impossible to fully realize. The mastery asymptote is a source of frustration. Why reach for something you can never attain? But it's also a source of allure. Why not reach for it? The joy is in the pursuit more than the realization. In the end mastery attracts precisely because mastery eludes. Superbly said, Mr. Daniel Pink. Thank you! This knowledge can make the difference between quitting and staying on track.

I recently read another book by Steven Kotler called *The Rise of Superman: Decoding the Science of Ultimate Human Performance.* This book (sort of) disputes the Anders Ericsson approach, and suggests that there is a faster way to acquire expertise. Actually it does not so much dispute the basic premise, as it argues that there is a way of speeding up the entire process. A least, that's how I have understood it.

I will confess, my jaw dropped, and kept dropping as I read this book. I kept saying to myself: This is the future. This is the future. Something big and important is happening here. Here is an entirely new breed of trailblazers, pushing the human race forward.

The premise of the book is that there is a (highly elusive) state of being (an optimal state of body) called the flow state. This is a wonderful state, and one in which our ability to perform is maximized. Put differently, if two competitors in any field of contest have the same level of skill, fitness, talent, etc., and both have equally prepared for the contest, then the competitor more completely able to enter the flow state for the entire duration of the contest is more likely to win the contest.

The task the author has given himself is to scientifically decode this flow state.

Indeed I have been so taken up by this book and the argument that deliberate practice in the flow state is the optimal route toward acquiring expertise, that I will devote an entire chapter to flow toward the end of the book and suggest that every PS&ST should strive to get into the flow state whenever engaging in PS&ST.

In one sentence, when practicing to improve performance, there is an optimal zone to practice in, and this zone is between boredom and anxiety.

I recently had a splendid discussion about these ideas with Ash. Ash requested that I go over all of this once again, this time with parents present. I met with all three of them and we agreed that Ash's project plan must be modified to include fitness routines and that all activities must be based on purposeful or deliberate practice.

Final thought: I suspect that in all aspects of life, in any endeavor that we want to excel in, we focus a bit too much on the endeavor itself, and a little too little on the fitness factor and not enough on the actual way in which we acquire expertise. I hope this makes some sense to you. In the final analysis, the fact that the South African rugby team won the World Cup may have been determined more by their advantage in fitness, rather than by their advantage in skill and talent.

Chapter 7

The Fear
of Public
Speaking

*"There are two types of speakers: Those that
are nervous and those that are liars."*
— *Mark Twain*

I've heard it many times, way too many times. *The Fear of
Public Speaking is Greater than the Fear of Death.*

My reactions have changed over the years from "This is
humorous, I should remember the line," to "sort of cute and
quaint, but not really true," to "oh no … not again," to "what
utter rubbish!"

So I will unequivocally state my thinking. The proclamation
"The Fear of Public Speaking is Greater than the Fear of Death,"
is utter rubbish. Or to restate this diplomatically, the assertion
is simply not true. And this one statement, this urban myth,
has probably done more disservice to aspiring public speakers,
those genuinely desiring to take the first step, than I care to
think about.

Do you, dear reader, fear death less than you fear having to
speak in public? Really? Please may I ask you again? Do you
fear death less than you fear public speaking? Really? Truly?

I do not deny that the fear of public speaking is very real. It
is. I have experienced its overpowering presence occasionally,
and know that in the future, I will have to cope with it
occasionally. I acknowledge that for some it can be debilitating,
even crippling. No, I do not disrespect it or deny it at all.

Some of the most compelling speeches I have ever heard
are those given by a speaker who is experiencing real fear
while speaking, and yet speaking anyway.

Case in Point: TED Talk by Megan Washington titled, "Why
I live in mortal dread of public speaking." In this talk, it is clear
that everyone in the audience is on Megan Washington's side.
How can they not be? This is the very definition of courage
right before our own eyes. *(The original definition of courage*

when it first came into the English language — it's from the Latin word cor, meaning heart—was to tell the story of who you are with your whole heart—Brené Brown, TED Talk). How can we not be filled with admiration? How can we not cheer this speaker on? (http://www.ted.com/talks/megan_washington_why_i_live_in_mortal_dread_of_public_speaking)

Let's take this a step further. I have been coached by Sandra Zimmer and have read her book *It's Your Time to Shine: How to Overcome Fear of Public Speaking, Develop Authentic Presence and Speak from Your Heart* many times. The reason I have read it many times is not because I have any abnormal fear of public speaking, but because I felt I had stumbled onto the work of a trailblazer. I kept having this feeling "she is onto something here" ... "she is onto something right here." This will one day be validated by new knowledge and by science. The wannabe detective in me was triggered. She reflects, that after having coached thousands of people, over decades, she has observed that those who start out with the most stage fright have the potential to be the most compelling speakers. Frequently they do end up being the most compelling speakers. I dare say that the Megan Washington TED Talk makes this case compellingly. Indeed the first chapter of Zimmer's book is titled *Congratulations, You've Got Stage Fright.*

Zimmer's coaching and method focus on getting the body fully prepared for the necessary work of public speaking; on getting into an "optimal state of body." Of course there is much more to her coaching, but to my mind, this is its most unique and valuable offering.

So if you feel the fear of public speaking is one you must confront or overcome, you cannot go wrong picking up this book. It has my high recommendation. There are nice short videos on her website too articulating just this.

No, I do not deny or disrespect stage fright or the very real and ubiquitous fear of public speaking—not at all.

A task I am giving myself in this chapter is to put distance, a lot of distance, between these two statements:

Statement One: The fear of public speaking is very real and it is universal. (TRUE)

Statement Two: The fear of public speaking is greater than the fear of death. (FALSE)

I've probably heard Statement Two five to ten times more frequently than I've heard Statement One. Indeed, I recently did a fantastic memory workshop and there too, when the trainer was teaching methods for remembering speeches, I heard the same old song. What a pity. It all sounded so genuine and real. As if there were real surveys and this was based on real data. It's just plain wrong. An unfortunate urban myth.

Believing that *The Fear of Public Speaking is Greater than the Fear of Death* is true does not help anyone. This statement is best removed from the vocabulary and thinking of public speaking, public speakers, and aspiring public speakers. Again, are you more afraid of public speaking than you are of death? For real?

Where did this nonsense (Statement Two, not Statement One) originate?

Statement Two seems to have been spread mainly from three sources: Comedians Jay Leno, Jerry Seinfeld and the 1977 *Book of Lists*

The Book Of Lists (which has sourced its content from Sunday Times, London (Oct 7, 1973)) gives us a list in response to:

"What are you most afraid of?" a team of market researchers asked 3,000 U.S. inhabitants. Many named more than one fear:

1. ***Speaking before a group (41%)***
2. *Heights (32%)*
3. *Financial problems (22%)*

3. *Insects and bugs (22%)*
3. *Deep water (22%)*
6. **Death (19%)**
6. *Sickness (19%)*
8. *Flying (18%)*
9. *Loneliness (14%)*
10. *Dogs (11%)*
11. *Driving/riding in a car (9%)*
12. *Darkness (8%)*
12. *Elevators (8%)*
14. *Escalators (5%)*

As Jay Leno quipped, *"I guess we'd rather be in the casket than delivering the eulogy."*

And here's a famous version from Jerry Seinfeld.

According to most studies, people's number one fear is public speaking. Death is number two. Does that seem right? That means to the average person, if you have to go to a funeral, you're better off in the casket than doing the eulogy.

From a comedian's laugh line, this assertion has been transformed to the status of a believed truth. What a pity. What next? People are more afraid of heights, insects and bugs, financial problems, deep water and sickness than they are afraid of death? Enough said!

This article gives more detail toward debunking the myth: http://tmvision.org/speaking/people-fear-public-speaking-death

Clearly there is a fear of public speaking. This fear is a common and universal one (Statement One). That being said, public speaking and oratory have been around for thousands of years. Millions of people have spoken publically. Surely any aspiring speaker can do the same. Surely every engineer and every project manager can do the same.

Anyway, what causes this fear? And how can we manage it?

Turns out that this fear is an evolutionary bequeath, triggered by ancient parts of our brains, responding to perceived threats. The trigger is founded more on the "Public," than on the "Speaking." The trigger is the observation of the subconscious mind that the attention of a lot of other people is on the speaker. This is the same trigger associated with any public appearance or performance, be it singing, or acting, or competing in sports.

Here are a couple of more detailed and authoritative explanations from two credible sources: TED-Ed and Psychology Today.

The science of stage fright (and how to overcome it)— Mikael Cho

https://www.youtube.com/watch?v=K93fMnFKwfI
or

The Science of Stage Fright: TED Blog

http://blog.ted.com/2013/10/16/required-watching-for-any-ted-speaker-the-science-of-stage-fright/comment-page-2/

A similar explanation comes from Psychology Today. If you have online access, it is much better to read this online. If not here is the content.

http://www.psychologytoday.com/blog/the-real-story-risk/201211/the-thing-we-fear-more-death

The Thing We Fear More Than Death

Why predators are responsible for our fear of public speaking (Published on Nov 28, 2012 by Glenn Croton, PhD in "The Real Story of Risk")

Surveys about our fears commonly show fear of public speaking at the top of the list. Our fear of standing up in front of a group and talking is so great that we fear it more than death, in surveys at least. On one hand I understand, having sweated myself about getting up in front of a group. On the other hand, it seems odd that we're so afraid—what are we afraid of, anyway? What do we think will happen to us? We're unlikely to suffer any real or lasting harm—or are we? The answer seems to lie in our remote past, in our evolution as social animals.

Humans evolved over the last few million years in a world filled with risks like large predators and starvation. Based on the fossil evidence of predator attacks on our human ancestors (as described in the book "Man the Hunted" written by Robert Sussman and Donna Hart), and on predation rates on large primates today, early humans were probably commonly hunted by a wealth of large predators. One common defense to predation displayed by primates and other animals is to live in groups. In a group, other group members can alert each other to predators and help to fight them off. The advantages of living in a group probably are the reason why early humans and other large primates evolved to be social, and why we are still social today.

Humans were not the largest, fastest, or fiercest animal —early humans survived by their wits and their ability to collaborate. Those that worked together well, helping others in their group, probably survived and passed on traits that contributed to social behavior.

Failure to be a part of the social group, getting kicked out, probably spelled doom for early humans. Anything that threatens our status in our social group, like the threat of ostracism, feels like a very great risk to us.

"Ostracism appears to occur in all social animals that have been observed in nature," said Kip Williams, a professor of *psychological sciences at Purdue who has studied ostracism. "To my knowledge, in the animal kingdom, ostracism is not only a form of social death, it also results in death. The animal is unable to protect itself against predators, cannot garner enough food, etc., and usually dies within a short period of time."*

The fear is not just about public speaking, but is also faced by many others who are faced with getting in front of a crowd and performing like athletes, actors, and musicians. As a social psychologist, teacher, and a sufferer of social anxiety, Dr. Signe Dayhoff suffered through intense fear of public speaking every time he got up to teach a class. "My tongue stuck to the roof of my dry mouth and I couldn't swallow, I blushed, sweated and trembled," he said. Eventually it got so bad that it interfered in his ability to do his job. Getting help, he found he could deal with the situation better. "As I recovered 12 years ago, using cognitive-behavior therapy, patience, persistence, and practice, I found that nearly 20 million individuals at any one time suffer from some form of social anxiety. They fear being negatively evaluated in anything they do; fear being rejected; fear being abandoned."

When faced with standing up in front of a group, we break into a sweat because we are afraid of rejection. And at a primal level, the fear is so great because we are not merely afraid of being embarrassed, or judged. We are afraid of being rejected from the social group, ostracized and left to defend ourselves all on our own. We fear ostracism still so much today it seems, fearing it more than death, because not so long ago getting kicked out of the group probably really was a death sentence.

To sum up:
1. Stage fright is triggered by an ancient part of our brain, which registers threat when receiving attention from large groups.
2. Stage fright results from the primal fear of being

ostracized from a group as a result of being judged unfavorably by that group.

3. Stage fright is the fight-or-flight response activated.
4. Stage fright can be managed. It has been managed for thousands of years, by millions of speakers.
5. The notion that the fear of public speaking is greater than the fear of death is an unfortunate myth, with unfortunate staying power, resulting from a misunderstood list and a couple of laugh lines.

I hope all of the above will allow you to put some distance between Statement One and Statement Two. Between truth and urban legend.

To the reader, to the project manager who needs to be an effective speaker, to the engineer who can only benefit by being an effective presenter and persuader, I am suggesting that if you anticipate experiencing stage fright, or experience stage fright, the first thing to do is not study techniques and methods to cope, but to decide, absolutely decide, that stage fright will not impede your PS&ST voyage.

Deciding to manage the fear of public speaking is probably more difficult, and certainly more essential, that the actual managing of fear.

Let me return to an argument I made in chapter 3 based around this quotation: *It is harder to decide—really and truly decide—to become a millionaire, than it is to actually become a millionaire.* A modified version of this quotation would be: *It is probably harder to decide—really and truly decide—to overcome the fear of public speaking, than it is to actually overcome the fear of public speaking.* I am not offering this as an exact science type of statement, but more as a means of recognizing that these are two very different things.

Truthfully, I think that the goal, "I will overcome the fear of public speaking" may not be optimal. There is no telling when this fear will show up. There's no telling when the fight-or-flight response will get activated. There's no telling when the fear of being judged or ostracized will surface. A better goal may be. "I will learn and use processes and techniques that will help me manage the fear of public speaking as and when it does surface," or "I will practice and practice and practice, in front of audiences, till I become more and more comfortable within my body when speaking in public."

And in the event that managing this fear on a regular basis turns out to be harder than expected, think about this from the late actress Helen Hayes. Befriend your fear, say "hello old friend" to yourself every time it does show up. And let it remind you; motivate you, to prepare even more.

"Fear is not a foe but a friend—a familiar companion that nagged me to do my best. Don't think of fear as a deterrent. It's a kick in the rear to prepare." — Helen Hayes, *First Lady of American Theatre*

Once you've committed to managing and befriending this famous fear, (the harder part) then proceed with whatever techniques work for you (the easier part):

— Meditating
— Listening to music
— Deep Breathing
— Exercising in the morning
— Moving your body—dancing or similar
— Power posing (http://www.ted.com/talks/amy_cuddy_your_body_language_shapes_who_you_are)
— Moving focus away from yourself to your audience
— Being thoroughly prepared
— Arranging for friends / support in the audience.
— Prepare, prepare, prepare
— Practice, practice, practice

— Visualize yourself on stage, feeling whatever you are feeling, and proceeding to do a splendid job nonetheless
— Make your own Pre-Speech Check List or Notes (see mine in Appendix 4, page 286)

Darren LaCroix, a world-class public speaker, entrepreneur, and coach extraordinaire, sums it up accurately in this mantra *"Stage time, stage time, stage time."*

Here is another Sun Tzu modification that may help you along the way. *Know your glossophobia (fear of public speaking), and know your speech thoroughly, and in a hundred speeches you will never be in peril.*

I have learned to prepare for stage fright, confident that mostly it will be minor and manageable—and it has been. Yet every now and then, it comes on with a fleeting ferocity and suddenness that I will do well to acknowledge, recognize, and cope with. The symptoms are different. Most recently it has been (1) a pounding chest, and (2) a shaking laser pointer beam.

Now I watch it, experience it, try and study it. I regularly ask for feedback from my audience, especially after one of these increasingly rare bouts, and know, basis this feedback, that my audience did not notice any of it.

The engineer in me thinks of my body as an engine with lots of mechanical, electrical, and chemical processes occurring simultaneously, in a biological context. It is my responsibility to tune this engine and to make it function optimally—not anyone else's.

Sometimes I think of stage fright as an excess of stress chemicals that has been set in circulation in my body—a neurobiological evolutionary bequeath/glitch of sorts. Any generic stress management technique may be effective in helping reduce this fear. Below is a list of stress management habits I have compiled over the last few years. It is worthwhile noting that these habits also result in increased willpower. These habits are, however, not the same thing as pre-speech preparation. These are exercises and routines that must be done on a regular basis, for a lifetime, whether you are speaking in public or not. They help with lots of life's general challenges by reducing the dominance of stress chemicals in my body. Tweaking and tuning the engine that is my body and me.

Building a few of these options into daily routines will probably help with the fear of public speaking, too.

— Breathing slowly and deeply (one to two minutes every hour: maximum three breaths per minute)
— Meditation (any attention training: spiritual or secular)
— Regular, healthy sleep
— Nature walk
— Good conversations
— Excellent and loving relationships
— Gardening
— Dancing
— Poetry
— Music (deliberate relaxing by deep listening, as opposed to zoning out)
— Singing
— Playing a musical instrument (http://ed.ted.com/lessons/how-playing-an-instrument-benefits-your-brain-anita-collins)
— Watching inspirational or motivational video clips
— Any flow-generating activities
— Focus on gratitude: especially first thing in the morning and last thing at night
— Mental exercises (crosswords, Sudoku, Lumosity games)

A task I set out to accomplish in this chapter is to put distance between these two statements:

Statement One: The fear of public speaking is very real and it is universal. (TRUE)

Statement Two: The fear of public speaking is greater than the fear of death. (FALSE)

Let's recap and recommit.

Statement Two = WRONG!

Statement One = TRUE. The fear of public speaking is as real as the fight-or-flight response is real. This is biology at work—really. The fear of public speaking is as real as the fear of being judged and being ostracized is real. Think Edgar Allan Poe. Think *"Only this and nothing more."*

This "I will overcome the fear of public speaking" is a suboptimal commitment.

These may be better commitment options:

— I will learn and use processes and techniques that will help me manage the fear of public speaking as and when it does surface.

— I will practice and practice and practice, in front of audiences, until I become more and more comfortable within my body when speaking in public.

— I will build stress management best practices into my daily routine.

This kind of thinking may help:

— "I am afraid of public speaking" can be converted to "I am experiencing fear in my body. This is natural and it will pass." The first statement makes it seem like a permanent condition. The second statement recognizes that it is a temporary condition.

— "Every day (even right now) thousands of people are

speaking in public—so can I."

Taking this thinking a step further, "I am experiencing fear in my body" can be converted into more specific thoughts and observations:

— I am experiencing sweaty and clammy palms.
— I am experiencing breathlessness.
— I feel my body going rigid.
— I am experiencing tightness in my throat.
— I am experiencing dryness of my tongue.
— I am experiencing wobbly and shaking knees.
— I am experiencing shaking hands.
— I am experiencing a pounding chest.
— I am experiencing knots or butterflies in my stomach.
— I am feeling flushes in my face—feeling red in my face.
    Welcome to our club! These are all (and nothing more than) "fight or flight response" related sensations.

It may be best to come up with your own rondo statement and alternate it between the above. I sometime use this as my rondo statement.

Only this and nothing more. This too shall pass. I am here to serve! This presentation is not about me.

Now it feels very different and much better.

— I am experiencing sweaty and clammy palms.
    Only this and nothing more. This too shall pass. I am here to serve! This presentation is not about me.
— I am experiencing breathlessness.
    Only this and nothing more. This too shall pass. I am here to serve! This presentation is not about me.
— I feel my body going rigid.
    Only this and nothing more. This too shall pass. I am here to serve! This presentation is not about me.

And so on.

If the fear still remains overpowering and unmanageable, consider this approach. Give up! Let the thoughts and fears run wild and listen to them. There is some serious emerging science here. For more on this give-up approach, check out chapter 9 of the book *The Willpower Instinct: How Self-Control Works, Why It Matters, and What You Can Do to Get More of It* by Kelly McGonigal, Ph.D.

Here is a brief explanation. Apparently it is very difficult "not to think" about something, once you've been instructed not to think about it.

This is sometime called the white bear problem. When Russian novelist Leo Tolstoy was young he had been told by his older brother to sit in a corner until he could stop thinking about a white bear. His brother returned much later to discover Leo still in the corner, paralyzed by his inability to stop thinking about a white bear.

Daniel Wegner, a Harvard psychologist, went on to study this white bear problem, experimenting with many students, and dubbed this effect *ironic rebound*. It seems that trying to eliminate a thought or an emotion can trigger this rebound, because of the way our brains handle "not to" commands. The brain splits this command into two parts. One part is tasked with directing your attention to anything but the prohibited thought. This part is called the operator. Another part of your mind is checking to see if you are indeed thinking what you are not supposed to be thinking. This process is called the monitor. The operator is enabled by the brain's hardware and software for self-control; it is deliberate, and it requires a good deal of mental resources and energy. Unlike the operator, the monitor is more closely related to the brain's threat-detection system and runs automatically without much mental effort.

Under ordinary circumstances the operator and monitor work in parallel and in cooperation. When mental resources are available and high, the operator does its job. When mental resources are not readily available, when you are tired, or stressed, or distracted (alcohol, illness, etc.) the operator cannot do its job.

From the book:

How can you find your way out of this dilemma? Wegner suggests that an antidote to ironic rebound is: Give up. When you stop trying to control unwanted thoughts and emotions, they stop controlling you.

If you have a very high anxiety when it comes to public speaking, consider studying chapter 9 of the book *The WILLPOWER Instinct* very sincerely.

I reiterate my basic argument: *It is probably harder to decide—really and truly decide—to overcome the fear of public speaking, than it is to actually overcome the fear of public speaking.* Once you've decided, really and truly decided, to overcome/manage/cope with/confront the fear of public speaking ... you've done your bit. Help will come! Help will come! Have patience. Have unyielding faith. Nothing less will do!

Another option. Every time you feel anxiety overtaking you when thinking about an upcoming presentation or speech, view it as an attention challenge. By default, your attention has been captured by ancient hardware and software. You have the option and capability of deliberately directing your attention to something else. Yes, attention training is required, but it can be done. If you view the onset of anxiety as a trigger, then you can immediately follow up with a planned response. For example, play a song. And give that song your full attention. And when attention wanders away from the song, gently bring it back to the song with loving-kindness to yourself. This is no more than a standard meditation practice. A song with supportive lyrics may be even more helpful. A suggestion; "If I Were Brave" by Jana Stanfield has wonderfully supportive lyrics. The goal here is to be able to convert default attention to deliberate attention at will. This is a benefit of regular meditation; the ability to keep bringing a wandering mind back to topic.

If all else fails, and I really and truly mean if **all else** fails, try this last-resort approach. All other approaches are better. Here is a scene from the movie *Invictus*. The championship game has just started and one player from the New Zealand team, Jonah Lomu, is dominating the South African team. The South African team captain calls for a huddle, *"Come boys. What the heck are we doing? Lomu is culling us. Forwards … we must start scrumming. We must disrupt him at the first phase … we can't allow Lomu to get the ball in space. He's freaking killing us. But listen … if Lomu gets the ball … whoever's there … James … Joost … hit the fucking guy … hold onto him … hold him. Help will come. Help will be there."*

Have a similar huddle and conversation with yourself. Face down your nemesis, glossophobia, the way champion rugby teams face powerful opponents. Help will come. Help will be there; especially if you are a member of a Toastmasters club. Help will come. Everyone in these clubs has faced and will continue to face glossophobia. You are not alone! Do not grant glossophobia permission to be a power that is freaking killing the best version of you. Don't let this happen.

Good luck! You have us on your side.

Modify this Eleanor Roosevelt quote and say it out loud: *"Nobody can make you feel inferior without your consent."* **"No one can make me feel frozen (by the fear of public speaking) without my consent."** Say it to your sponsor and to your support system. Print it out and stare at it—then stare it down. Help will come. Help will come.

Visualize glossophobia as an adversary with a definite shape and form, and when he/she becomes too disruptive to your life-plans, hit the f-ing guy. Help will come. Help will come.

Here is my *eighth wish* for you. "May you always see the very natural fear of public speaking for what it is: An Inevitable Bridge; not an Impregnable Wall."

Let's begin closing now. This is EXERCISE #7. Say this aloud. "Fear is a familiar friend—always reminding me to give my best."

"To give anything less than my best ... is to sacrifice my gifts."

And allow me to close out this chapter with one last message. If there is only one memo that remains from this chapter, let it be this: Once and for all, the correlation between Statement One and Statement Two is a joke.

Chapter 8

Ending Your Speech

"Begin with the end in mind."
Habit #2: The Seven Habits of Highly
Effective People by Stephen R Covey

I'll have to admit that Mr. Covey was probably not thinking much about speech craft when he articulated this habit, but it is intriguingly exact.

Here's a common and very important question: "What is the most important thing you should know and prepare for when writing and delivering a speech or presentation?" I have encountered many responses, most of them very compelling. They include:

— It's about your audience; know your audience and its needs.
— It's about the connection to, and the rapport with your audience.
— It's a strong opening.
— It's a strong ending.
— It is your humor, which entertains and enhances memory.
— It is brilliant transitions.
— It's a strong punch line.
— It's a very powerful and universal message.
— It's a mesmerizing personal story.
— It is an emotional roller coaster ride.
— It's the content.
— It's the delivery.

My pragmatic (& not theoretical) take is that the ending is perhaps the most important part of a speech. Here are some thoughts and stories to make the case. What follows are some arguments (and new knowledge) that persuaded me to focus very hard on the ending.

Argument 1: Have a memorable ending.

Let me state the obvious. You may as well not give a speech if no one **remembers** it at all.

None of the components of the speech matter at all (structure, content, transitions, opening, closing, carry-out messages, calls to action, ideas worth spreading, etc.) if nothing is remembered. Sounds obvious, but after listening to presentations like Nobel Prize winning psychologist Daniel Kahneman's, TED Talk "The riddle of experience vs. memory," it seems worth looking into a little bit more.

http://www.ted.com/talks/daniel_kahneman_the_riddle_of_experience_vs_memory

What we are looking at here is the nature of memory itself and questioning a default conclusion that memory is based entirely and accurately on experience. You remember what you experience. Right? For example, it would seem valid to conclude that if you enjoyed 15 or more minutes of a 20-minute speech you can expect to have a good memory of the speech. Turns out, this may not be so.

Here's a part of the Daniel Kahneman, TED Talk. *"Now, I'd like to start with an example of somebody who had a question-and-answer session after one of my lectures reported a story, and that was a story—He said he'd been listening to a symphony, and it was absolutely glorious music and at the very end of the recording, there was a dreadful screeching sound. And then he added, really quite emotionally, it ruined the whole experience. But it hadn't. What it had ruined were the memories of the experience. He had had the experience. He had had 20 minutes of glorious music. They counted for nothing because he was left with a memory; the memory was ruined, and the memory was all that he had gotten to keep."*

Couldn't this apply for any speech? Conclusion: Make a disproportionate effort to end your speech well, because how your speech is remembered, depends disproportionately on the end. This has more to do with the very nature of memory than it has to do with the nature of your speech. Make this disproportionate effort in the planning and crafting stages.

For a powerful reinforcement of this argument, check out the segment of the talk from minute 3:45 to minute 5:45. It is about two patients, one of whom clearly experienced more pain than the other, but ended up with a significantly less painful memory.

I think that science is discovering that memory is quite different from how we conventionally understand it. This makes more sense if we can accept that we all have an experiencing-self and a remembering-self ... and that these two selves are very different. It is worthwhile factoring this into your thinking and planning, when preparing a speech.

How your audience experiences your speech and how your audience remembers your speech could be very different.

As I was thinking about this, I wondered, "How do famous speeches end? Do they validate this argument?" And the answer I got was, "Not really; not always"

From the American Rhetoric website, Top 100 speeches. The top 2 speeches are

Number 1: Martin Luther King Jr.: I Have A Dream
Number 2: John Fitzgerald Kennedy: Inaugural Address

And here are their endings:

And when this happens, and when we allow freedom to ring, when we let it ring from every village and every hamlet, from every state and every city, we will be able to speed up that day when all of God's children, black men and white men, Jews and Gentiles, Protestants and Catholics, will be able to join hands and sing in the words of the old Negro spiritual: Free at last! Free at last! Thank God Almighty, we are free at last!

And ...

Finally, whether you are citizens of America or citizens of the world, ask of us here the same high standards of strength and sacrifice which we ask of you. With a good conscience our only sure reward, with history the final judge of our deeds, let us go forth to lead the land we love, asking His blessing and His help, but knowing that here on earth God's work must truly be our own.

While these are both phenomenal endings, they are not the most remembered parts of the speeches. *"I have a dream ..."* and *"Ask not what ..."* are the most remembered parts. I guess there are many explanations for this, including the tendency of modern mass communication to downsize to sound bites, and that the mythologization of great speeches has its own unique progression and logic. The most remembered parts of these speeches are the most often heard parts of the speeches.

What to conclude? At the very least, "do no harm" with your ending. Do not end in a *dreadful way that ruins the whole experience.* Even a small glitch, like running over time, getting stressed in the process, or having people beginning to leave prior completion of your talk, due to your (or the event) running overtime can result in the whole experience being ruined, or more accurately, the memory of the whole experience being short-changed. Do you agree?

Of even greater concern: A Q&A ending has the potential of ruining any speech, regardless how excellent it was. What if the audience only remembers "a dreadful screeching sound" as you fumble a question or two, or get into a less than optimal exchange with a questioner? That's unfortunate—even terrible. No, it is best never to end with Q&A. Yes, have a Q&A session, but control it tightly, with something like this. "Before I close, I can take three to four questions, for the next five minutes." Then as you are taking the last question add, "This will be the last question before I close," and finally transition to your closing by adding, "I'll close now with … and I will be available later to take more questions at the back of the room."

I am aware that many famous presenters and most ordinary speakers end with Q&A; indeed it is still the default practice. I am not saying it is wrong. What I am suggesting is that it is risky. The risk of ending with *a dreadful screeching sound that ruined the whole experience* is increased. Just beware of the possibility. The memory of the whole experience is heavily dependent on the ending of it. Everyone in your audience has two distinct selves, the experiencing self and the remembering self—and these two are very different.

Argument 2: Start with the last line in mind.

Toastmasters International, TED and MOTH are all very well-known PS&ST forums. Moth is a storytelling platform. Here is a guideline from the MOTH website.

Steer clear of meandering endings. They kill a story! **Your last line should be clear in your head before you start.** *Yes, bring the audience along with you as you contemplate what transpires in your story, but remember, you are driving the story, and must know the final destination. Keep your hands on the wheel!*

Good enough for MOTH: good enough for us.

Argument 3: Determine the audience's final emotion as the starting point of your speech preparation.

Vikas Jhingran is the 2007 Toastmasters International Contest World Champion of Public Speaking. He is an engineer and researcher with a doctorate from the Massachusetts Institute of Technology—quite unusual for recipients of this high honor. He has also been a project manager. This is a highly unusual background, and not surprisingly he brings a highly unusual approach and unusual insights to the world of PS&ST.

I have met Vikas Jhingran on a few occasions, attended his keynotes and breakout sessions; and have been on an organizing team for a PMI-H event where he has presented. When I heard he was writing a book, *Emote*, I immediately decided to buy it. Words like "paradigm shift," "seminal," "trailblazer," "new knowledge" kept coming to mind as I was reading the book.

He advocates an uncommon approach to speech writing in that he determines the "final emotion" as the starting point of his speech preparation. He decides exactly what emotion he wants his audience to be feeling at the end of his talk.

He then constructs the communication by building points (and transitions) keenly aware of the emotional interaction between speaker and audience. It is a very insightful and creative approach. Here are some sections of his book *Emote: Using Emotions to Make Your Message Memorable*, which I highlighted when reading.

In a speech, even though the words and ideas are going only from the speaker to the audience, there is always a back and forth of emotions.

As strange as it may sound, people just don't know what they are supposed to do when they get up and speak.

I developed a definition of a speech. I defined it as an "emotional rollercoaster ride for the speaker and the audience."

I felt that if I could successfully convey this final emotion to the audience, I would have delivered a good speech.

There are two important components that make a speech successful using this method. The first is understanding the emotions that need to be conveyed ... In my speeches, I 'live the emotions' I am trying to convey. This in itself is a very powerful concept ... The second component of the speech is the ability to take my audience on the emotional journey with me.

The truth is that at the end of a good speech, the audience only remembers how they feel.

A skilled speaker can link the specific purpose of a speech to a feeling, understand the basic emotions that cause the feeling, and then write a speech that generates these basic emotions.

A common source of confusion for someone beginning to prepare a new speech is "Where do I start?" The preparation of the speech begins at the end—with a clear understanding of what the final emotional state of the audience needs to be. This is the emotional state that the speaker would like the audience to be in at the end of the speech.

I also recommend that you check out his talk on YouTube and listen to this podcast to get a better appreciation of what his approach has to offer you.

Vikas Jhingran, "The Swami's Question": https://www.youtube.com/watch?v=mDaOWYCkvvc

Toastmasters podcast: http://www.toastmasterspodcast.com/index.php/rss-feed/105-toastmasters-podcast-079-emote-with-2007-world-champion-of-public-speaking-vikas-jhingran

I recommend that you procure *Emote*. It is unlike anything else I have encountered. It can confer a distinguishing advantage as you progress on your PS&ST voyage. And the author is an engineer and project manager.

To summarize this argument—begin writing your speech with the final emotion in mind.

Argument 4: Create neural resonance.

I will try and summarize the way I have understood some of the material of Daniel Goleman's book *Social Intelligence*. Imagine that two people set up neurobiological and other biometric feedback equipment, and allow themselves to be monitored. Imagine that these two people are alone, each minding their own business, doing their own thing. Certain brain activation patterns will be revealed. It is safe to assume that the brain activation patterns for these two people will be significantly different.

Now let's assume these two people walk toward each other and begin a conversation. Let's say that initially the conversation is tentative and halting. The brain activation patterns will remain different, but will gradually become less dissimilar.

As the conversation becomes better and better, as these two people tune more into each other, as these two people begin to agree more and more, as these two people begin to feel the same emotions, their body language will begin mirroring each other. If one leans in, the other will lean in; if one crosses arms, the other will cross arms, etc. It is like a synchronized mini-dance with mini-moves in fractions of seconds. Breathing patterns begin to mimic each other and synchronize. And the observed brain activation patterns will increasingly become more and more similar. When the brain patterns become very similar or even identical, this is called resonance. It is supposed to be a very nice feeling and is a foundation of successful relationships, even good health.

From Daniel Goleman's *"Social Intelligence: The New Science of Human Relationships"*: *Getting in synch can be a visceral pleasure* (This is biology!), *and the larger the group, the better ... When two people converse, we can see this emotional minuet being played out in the dance of flashing eyebrows, rapid hand*

143

gestures, fleeting facial expressions, swiftly adjusted word pacing, shift of gaze and the like. Such synchrony lets us mesh and connect and, if we do so well, feel a positive emotional resonance with the other person.

Isn't this what we are trying to do when speaking in public or when telling a story?

The more the synchrony occurs the more alike the emotions both partners will feel; getting in synch creates an emotional match.

While it may be very difficult to get an entire audience into neural resonance, for the entire duration of a speech, I believe this must be the ultimate objective. This is true for any type of speech—informational to inspirational—and everything in between.

And if we cannot get all the audience into neural resonance for the entire duration of the speech, at the very least we must aim to have the majority in neural resonance at the very end of the speech.

This means we must begin planning and crafting a speech with neural resonance as the end in mind. Neural resonance = the entire audience thinking the same thoughts and feeling the same emotions.

And the opening, the transitions, and the body must all be working hard to increase neural resonance on a continuous improvement basis.

Argument 5: Plan your speech with the deliverable in mind.

From one project manager to another, let me ask you this, "When a project is initially being conceived, what first comes to your mind?" The end result, the deliverable? Yes? In some parallel way, isn't this the same argument as "begin to write your speech with the end in mind?" Doesn't it make excellent sense to begin planning a speech with the deliverable in mind? What do I want my audience to know, think, do, and feel after listening to my speech? How can I make it most memorable? With a strong ending? What do I want my audience to be feeling when I close?

These five arguments have convinced me that the best way to **pragmatically** begin planning a speech or presentation is with the end in mind.

After you have committed to a speech get these basic questions answered:

1. What is the topic? What am I going to speak about?
2. Who is my audience?
3. What has my boss / customer / supplier / event planner asked me to speak about?

Next come the more important questions:

1. What do I want my audience to be feeling at the very end?
2. What do I want my audience to remember of this speech?
3. What do I want my audience to commit to after this speech?
4. What perspective of my audience do I want to change after this speech?
5. What is my call to action?

I strongly recommend that you do not proceed with writing out or preparing your speech unless you have got these questions partially or fully answered.

If you do not know very clearly what you want the audience to get out of your speech, how can they be expected get a clear message, a clear call to action, and a clear final emotion?

Here are some of the more common and effective speech closing techniques:
— Circular closing (using the same or similar sentence you used to open your speech, or calling back to some earlier part of your speech)
— Story or anecdote
— Quotation
— Call to action
— Rhetorical question
— Summary of main points
— Poetry

Here is EXERCISE #8. It is in two parts. One part is for one of your old speeches and one for some well-known speech.

Exercise 8a
Take out one of your old presentations, preferably one that you already analyzed in chapter 5 and look at the end again. Do you know what your audience will be thinking and feeling as soon as you complete your speech? Is this the final emotion and message you want to leave them with? If no, rework the end of the speech.

Exercise 8b
Take a look at some speeches and decide which strong endings you like and would like to use as a model. To decide which speeches to check out simply try and recall the endings, or more accurately, how you felt at the ending. The ones that you remember are the ones that had a strong emotional connection.

Here are some questions to use when checking out your speech conclusions. Use these questions as a checklist after you have drafted the end of your speech, and then again after you have finalized the conclusion.

— Feeling of closure achieved?
— Impactful?
— Any new points introduced? If yes, remove!
— No longer that 5%–10% of total speech time?
— Identify the closing technique: Circular (same as beginning)? Story? Quotation? Rhetorical question? Call to action? Summary? Poetry?
— Will I be experiencing the desired final emotion?
— Will my audience be feeling the desired final emotion?
— Will there be neural resonance?
— Will this ending be remembered? Really?

If you have a significant number of "yes" answers, you have got a good speech ending in place. If not, negotiate harder with yourself to work harder. Keep repeating until you are satisfied.

I recommend the Toastmasters resource, "Concluding Your Speech," which you can get for free if you are a member of Toastmasters. It is an excellent resource. Get it and go through it. It is in the format of a 10 –15 minute presentation. http://www.toastmasters.org/MainMenuCategories/ Shop/ManualsBooksVideosCDs_1/ProgramsModules/ TheBetterSpeakerSeries/271DCD.aspx

To close out this chapter, let me direct your attention to two famous speeches, with very memorable endings. One is a masterful example of a president of the US leaving his entire country with the same final emotion—creating neural resonance on vast scale. The speech by Ronald Reagan is called "The Space Shuttle Challenger Tragedy Address." The entire speech is a little over four minutes. Study the speech carefully and discover anew the power of a masterful speech closing:

http://www.americanrhetoric.com/speeches/
ronaldreaganchallenger.htm
https://www.youtube.com/watch?v=Qa7icmqgsow

Nothing ends here; our hopes and our journeys continue.

I want to add that I wish I could talk to every man and woman who works for NASA, or who worked on this mission and tell them: "Your dedication and professionalism have moved and impressed us for decades. And we know of your anguish. We share it."

There's a coincidence today. On this day three hundred and ninety years ago, the great explorer Sir Francis Drake died aboard ship off the coast of Panama. In his lifetime the great frontiers were the oceans, and a historian later said, "He lived by the sea, died on it, and was buried in it." Well, today, we can say of the Challenger crew: Their dedication was, like Drake's: complete.

The crew of the space shuttle Challenger honored us by the manner in which they lived their lives. We will never forget them, nor the last time we saw them, this morning, as they prepared for their journey and waved goodbye and "slipped the surly bonds of earth" to "touch the face of God."

The second speech closing that stayed with me for a very long time is from the 1994 Nelson Mandela inaugural address.

https://www.youtube.com/watch?v=grh03-NjHzc

We must therefore act together as a united people, for national reconciliation, for nation building, for the birth of a new world.

Let there be justice for all.

Let there be peace for all.

Let there be work, bread, water and salt for all.

Let each know that for each the body, the mind and the soul have been freed to fulfill themselves.

Never, never and never again shall it be that this beautiful land will again experience the oppression of one by another and suffer the indignity of being the skunk of the world.

Let freedom reign.

The sun shall never set on so glorious a human achievement!

God bless Africa!

Here is my *ninth wish* for you. "May all your speech and presentation closings generate total neural resonance."

Chapter 9

Leaders Are Speakers
(Rondo 1)

"Mend your speech a little, lest it may mar your fortunes."
— William Shakespeare: King Lear to his
youngest daughter Cordelia

The purpose of these rondo chapters is not to provide PS&ST content, but rather it is to:

1. Evangelize PS&ST to PM&Es. I intend to use new knowledge, new ideas, and real-world examples to accomplish this.

2. Motivate PM&Es to decide—really and truly decide—to commit (time and money) to PS&ST expertise. I intend to use new knowledge, new ideas, and real-world examples to accomplish this.

These are the primary objectives of this book; of this product.

Here are some **real-world examples** to contemplate.

Neither Shakespeare nor King Lear could have possibly imagined that centuries after their time, a man called Warren Buffet would be guided by a similar message. *Mend your (ability for public) speech a little, lest it mar your fortunes.*

There is a series of documentaries called *Bloomberg Game Changers*. One of the documentaries is on Warren Buffet. Mr. Buffett is one of the most successful, admired, respected, and famous investors of all time, and amongst the wealthiest people on the planet.

Here is a small section from this documentary, Warren Buffett Revealed: Bloomberg Game Changers (https://www. youtube.com/watch?v=GJ1MW-OR0tI&list=PLUqYZEKhvdm UJzr4I6fDkL_WPTWL7yU_U&index=6)

Armed with a grand philosophy, Buffet headed back to Omaha to start his own business. He formed the original partnership with seven or eight people. Convincing people beyond the first seven investors got rockier.

Buffet: My sales pitch wasn't very effective. I was twenty years old. I looked like I was about sixteen, and I probably behaved like I was about twelve. So I would go around and call on people. They were always nice to me. But I would see a Mr. Smith and I would go through all these facts and figures about why you should buy some stock. And when I got all through, in my head I would count to three, I would go one, two, three; and then Mr. Smith would say, "What does your Dad think?" and I would always want to hit him (laughs).

Narrator: It was frustrating. Buffett knew he had to be a better salesman. So he turned to popular self-help guru Dale Carnegie.

*Buffett: "Well, **I had to be able to communicate with people better; I mean in groups, particularly. I just knew that I just couldn't go through life terrified of public speaking** and I'd heard about the Dale Carnegie course."*

Narrator: And he applied those lessons when he began dating his hometown girl.

Buffett: "I mean, I proposed to my wife during the Dale Carnegie course, so (laughs) I mean I got my money's worth right during the course. I had the intellect to succeed, but I did not have the persona. I was not put together as a person until I met her.

Narrator: Buffett was finally ready to put his career in gear.

Here's a question that crossed my mind. If Warren Buffett had, on principle, refused to make a commitment (including time and money) to improve his public speaking skills, would he be where he is today? Of course any thoughts and opinions are just speculation and nothing more, yet I cannot but conclude—no, Warren Buffett may not have been where he is today had he not crossed a necessary bridge. Indeed he seems to be implying this himself.

One does not have to be a truly great communicator, public speaker, or storyteller to be a great leader, project manager or engineer, or for that matter a billionaire, but one has to be at least a very good communicator, speaker, or storyteller to realize one's **full potential**. At the very, very, least; one must be a good-enough communicator. Do you agree?

Dear Reader, you are a PM&E. By default you are an ambassador for our professions; there is no argument here. Others will judge our professions by the way we are. Period. Are you a good enough communicator? If no, isn't it reasonable to conclude that you will deny yourself access to the greatness within you? If no, isn't it reasonable to conclude that you will be a less than an optimal ambassador for our professions? If no, isn't it conceivable that some of your greatest gifts may end up in a graveyard? My request is that you take a very serious look at these questions.

As you have come this far in the book, you have already taken the first steps and made the first commitments, even if only tentative commitments, toward PS&ST expertise. If you indeed have a two-year (or more) project plan with time and money commitments—excellent. Nonetheless, sooner or later commitments and motivations waver. When, not if, this happens, I invite you to revisit this chapter and re-commit to either commencing or continuing your PS&ST voyage. And that means time and money.

My reading and viewing include a fair amount of biography and autobiography. Stories like Warren Buffet's are everywhere. There is a clear pattern of successful people being splendid communicators, yet somehow PS&ST does not seem to be accorded high status in the arsenal of essential knowledge of PM&Es as other subjects. This is a mystery to me.

Here are a couple more examples.

Both Bill Gates and the late Steve Jobs were pioneers

and legends of the personal computer era. Steve Jobs was, additionally, a pioneer of the computer-based devices era, and Bill Gates is additionally a pioneer in philanthropy. They have both secured places amongst the pantheon of greats.

We see the same pattern in a Bill Gates documentary, as we saw in the Warren Buffet documentary. The pattern being "communication made the difference; communication was the enabler."

From: The Bill Gates Documentary

https://www.youtube.com/watch?v=fO2u-uxVBIc

Bill Gates joins Lakeside High School—a top private school

Narrator: He began to blossom at Lakeside, making new friends and finding more challenging classes.

Fred Wright (Teacher): He was an excellent math student. He was excellent across the board. He was a superb drama student, and interested in reading all different kinds of books. **He wasn't just math- and science-oriented. He had a wide breadth of interests.**

Later in the documentary (minute 18:45) At the end of 1978 with sales approaching the one million mark, they moved Microsoft from Albuquerque to Seattle. Bill was glad to be back and went into high gear to promote his hometown company. **It was Bill Gates who was actually the real marketing genius behind Microsoft.** *Early on he was the one who was actually going out on the road and trying to sell his company and his software.*

Fast forward to 1995 when Windows 95 was released (minute 37:45). Again the same commentary. **"Clearly Bill Gates was still Microsoft's best salesman."**

When you think of Bill Gates, do you think "best salesman?" Do you think "super communicator?" If not, why not? Another question that crossed my mind: Would Microsoft have become what it is, had Bill Gates not been a super-effective communicator? These are relevant and valid questions to ponder.

Most people already know what an outstanding speaker (mesmerizer may be a more accurate word) Steve Jobs was. He famously persuaded many listeners with his reality distortion field. He reinvented the product launch and brought a burning enthusiasm for his products to his keynotes. In characteristic Steve Jobs style, he reinvented the keynote. Books have been written about his presentation secrets. His videos on YouTube have been viewed millions of time. Steve Jobs was a phenomenal speaker who used storytelling masterfully.

Same questions again. When you think of Steve Jobs, do you think "best salesman?" Do you think "super communicator?" If no, why not? Do you think Apple would have become what it is, had Steve Jobs not been a super-effective communicator? These are relevant and valid questions to ponder.

Here is yet another question that comes to my mind. Granted, any answer is pure speculation; nonetheless no harm done in contemplating the question anyway. If somehow either of these individuals started out by being "not-good-enough" communicators, and neither cared to work on their PS&ST skills, would the PC and (computer-based) devices landscape be different? I think it likely.

Turning this question around, is it possible to imagine that there were other, even many PM&Es, with the same level of engineering prowess and talents as Gates and Jobs, who were not good-enough communicators and PS&ST, (who stubbornly opted not to improve) and as a result of this, the world has lost many engineering and consumer marvels? I think it is likely. Is it realistic to wonder if much of the genius of the "not good enough" communicators amongst the masses of PM&Es is destined for the graveyard?

If you agree, even partially, with this line of thinking, then shouldn't we evangelize PS&ST for PM&Es right from the college level? It seems totally necessary to me.

Why don't you watch a few Warren Buffet, Bill Gates, and Steve Jobs talks now, and study these real-world examples to see if you can learn anything. Let their examples convince you that being anything less than a good-enough PS&ST is to sacrifice your gifts. "Good enough" is not a low standard here. It is a high bar, which requires commitment, knowledge, disciplined practice, and feedback.

Sometime in the future, consider evangelizing PS&ST to future PM&Es, especially young students. Thanks in advance.

Chapter 10

Opening Your Speech

"You never get a second chance to make a first impression."

Even though this quotation is very familiar, indeed very clichéd, it is nonetheless very true. Ignore it at your own peril. Devoting a lot of thought and planning to your speech opening is a necessary, indeed excellent approach.

In chapter 8, I have stated that from a pragmatic point of view, I consider the closing of the speech to be the most important. That is where I start my speech writing and that is where I recommend you start yours. I have laid out detailed and multiple arguments explaining why I have opted for this approach. I certainly did not start out my PS&ST voyage with this approach. I wish I had.

That being said, I will 100% agree that there is no one correct approach for everyone, so please feel free to disagree, and to select the approach that works best for you.

Many prefer to start writing their speeches at the beginning and I would not argue much against such an approach. Again, do whatever works best for you; simultaneously remain flexible and bold.

Here are some heuristics and thoughts commonly associated with opening a speech:

- The audience will decide whether they like you in the first 7 seconds. Keeping it practical, know that your likeability will be determined in the first 5 to 10 seconds. Losing your audience at this stage is a crippling disadvantage. You will have to work extra hard to recover, so get this critical bit of your speech right.
- Additionally, be aware that a lot of research is pointing to the fact people make snap judgments about likeability, trustworthiness, and competence in a fraction of a second, even in a 10th of a second. You may be familiar with some of these studies where photographs of

competing politicians were shown to college students for a 10th of a second, and their snap impressions of the more likeable, trustworthy, and competent politician's face accurately reflected the outcome of the election.

- The audience will decide, subconsciously or otherwise, whether they are interested in your subject, and in listening further, in 30–35 seconds. This is your window of opportunity to capture their interest and attention. If you utilize this time skillfully, you will be in an optimal position to win your audience's agreement and support. I find the analogy to a plane's fuel consumption intriguing, and worth considering. A plane consumes much more fuel during takeoff than at any other time. *(I understand: For a 1.8 hour flight, the MD80 burns half of the fuel required for the flight from takeoff to level off. Fuel flow on takeoff roll is about 30,000 lb/hour. Fuel flow in cruise is about 13,000 lb/hour.)* I feel a speaker cannot go wrong by devoting a similarly high ratio of energy and planning to a strong opening.

- It is worth thinking that your speech actually begins well before you start speaking, indeed before you even get onto the stage. Your audience will be judging you, evaluating you, from the minute they set eyes on you and know that you are the speaker. How you walk up to the stage, how you gather and compose yourself before your first words, how you energize yourself and the audience before your first words matter significantly. They matter more than most speakers are aware. One of the most cited walk-ups prior to actually speaking is Barack Obama's 2004 DNC Speech. Check out the first few seconds of this clip, https://www.youtube.com/watch?v=

OFPwDe22CoY "The Speech that Made Obama President."

- If the speaker has captured an audience's attention and interest, if the audience intently wants to hear more, feels connected to the speaker and likes the speaker, then the opening can be judged as successful.

Here is a checklist I use when reviewing the opening of my speeches, or when helping others with their speeches. Will this opening:

- Introduce the topic?
- Capture the attention of the audience?
- Establish some connection and rapport with the audience?
- Have the audience thinking, "I like this speaker?"
- Have the audience thinking, "Keep going: don't stop," "tell me more?"
- Have the audience thinking, "The speaker is just like me?"
- Be constrained between 5%–10 % of the time?

A few ineffective (some surprisingly common) ways to start a speech are:

- A lengthy greeting. Greetings and acknowledgements are best inserted as transitions from a strong opening to the speech body.
- A weather report. What a wonderful day, etc. These statements contribute absolutely nothing to a speech, and they unnecessarily shrink the window of opportunity to capture the audience's attention. The only reason why speakers still open with these sorts of comments is out of habit or expectation, i.e. I am expected to start with this; because everyone else starts this way. This thinking belongs to the past. At best this is a safe

opening. I recommend you be bold with your openings.

- I haven't really had a chance to prepare. I did not have enough notice ... etc. True or not, don't say it. It contributes absolutely nothing.

- An apology. Sorry, I am late. Sorry, the technology is not working. Sorry about the room not being ready, etc. Do not start with an apology. Period. If an apology is called for, or is appropriate, insert it as a transition. Keep it brief, be genuine and humble, and move on. Your task as a speaker is to inform, educate, entertain, persuade, inspire, etc. Devote yourself fully to the task at hand. This is the best way of respecting the audience's presence and time.

- Do not start with a whimper, with hesitation, with your attention drawn inward. Start with a bang! Almost always, your audience is on your side and wants you to succeed. Don't let them down.

Remember, this is the window of opportunity. The first impression has disproportionate consequences.

Some of the more common and more modern openings are:

- Start with a story or anecdote (increasingly, this is becoming one of the most popular openings).

- Start with a rhetorical question, or even a series of open-ended questions—all of which point in one direction.

- Start with a bold statement, a startling statement or a shocking statistic.

- An immediate introduction of the topic and a road map or a guidepost. Today I want to talk about ...

Some examples:
Story or Anecdote
TED Talk: Aimee Mullins: My twelve pairs of legs
http://www.ted.com/talks/aimee_mullins_prosthetic_

aesthetics

I was speaking to a group of about 300 kids, ages six to eight, at a children's museum, and I brought with me a bag full of legs, similar to the kinds of things you see up here, and had them laid out on a table for the kids. And, from my experience, you know, kids are naturally curious about what they don't know, or don't understand, or is foreign to them. They only learn to be frightened of those differences when an adult influences them to behave that way, and maybe censors that natural curiosity, or you know, reins in the question-asking in the hopes of them being polite little kids. So I just pictured a first-grade teacher out in the lobby with these unruly kids, saying, "Now, whatever you do, don't stare at her legs."

But, of course, that's the point. That's why I was there, I wanted to invite them to look and explore. So I made a deal with the adults that the kids could come in without any adults for two minutes on their own. The doors open, the kids descend on this table of legs, and they are poking and prodding, and they're wiggling toes, and they're trying to put their full weight on the sprinting leg to see what happens with that.

And I said, "Kids, really quickly. I woke up this morning, I decided I wanted to be able to jump over a house—nothing too big, two or three stories—but, if you could think of any animal, any superhero, any cartoon character, anything you can dream up right now, what kind of legs would you build me?"

And immediately a voice shouted, "Kangaroo!" "No, no, no! Should be a frog!" "No. It should be Go Go Gadget!" "No, no, no! It should be the Incredibles." And other things that I don't— aren't familiar with. And then, one 8-year-old said, "Hey, why wouldn't you want to fly too?" And the whole room, including me, was like, "Yeah."

Transition from opening story to main message:

(Laughter) And just like that, I went from being a woman

that these kids would have been trained to see as "disabled" to somebody that had potential that their bodies didn't have yet. Somebody that might even be super-abled. Interesting.

Let's take this opening through our checklist. Your answers and opinions may be different from mine, and that's OK.

- Did the speaker introduce the topic? *Yes: prosthetics and disability reimagined.*
- Did the speaker capture the attention of the audience? *100% for me.*
- Did the speaker establish some connection and rapport with the audience? *100% for me. I felt an instant admiration and respect for the speaker.*
- Did the speaker have the audience thinking, "I like this speaker"? *100% for me. Even more than like, I felt admiration and respect.*
- Did the speaker have the audience thinking, "Keep going: don't stop" "tell me more?" *100% for me.*
- Did the speaker have the audience thinking, "The speaker is just like me?" *Sort of. More accurately, I remember thinking, if I faced similar adversity, I would like to think this is how I would face the world.*
- Did the speaker constrain the opening between 5–10 % of the time? *No—340 words out of a total of 1465 words = 23%. As far a time goes, opening was 2 minutes of a total of 10 minutes = 20%. But still very effective— and set the stage for the rest of the talk brilliantly.*

Open-ended questions.
TED Talk: Simon Sinek: How great leaders inspire action. http://www.ted.com/talks/simon_sinek_how_great_leaders_inspire_action

As of this writing this talk has been viewed more than 20 million times on the TED site. It is a very popular and successful talk.

The opening is a masterful example of multiple questions, all of which point to the same direction.

How do you explain when things don't go as we assume? Or better, how do you explain when others are able to achieve things that seem to defy all of the assumptions? For example:

Why is Apple so innovative? Year after year, after year, after year, they're more innovative than all their competition. And yet, they're just a computer company. They're just like everyone else. They have the same access to the same talent, the same agencies, the same consultants, the same media. Then why is it that they seem to have something different?

Why is it that Martin Luther King led the Civil Rights Movement? He wasn't the only man who suffered in a pre-civil rights America, and he certainly wasn't the only great orator of the day. Why him?

And why is it that the Wright brothers were able to figure out controlled, powered man flight when there were certainly other teams who were better qualified, better funded ... and they didn't achieve powered man flight, and the Wright brothers beat them to it.

There's something else at play here.

Simon Sinek then transitions into his big idea, which is the common answer to these three questions. His big idea is that these inspiring examples (Apple, King, Wright brothers) communicated in a different way from the rest of us. He codifies this in a Golden Circle—with the Why? How? What? questions being asked in a different sequence.

Let's take this opening through our checklist. Your answers and opinions may be different from mine, and that's OK.

- Did the speaker introduce the topic? *Not really. Did not intend to yet. But is clearly pointing the way to his big idea.*

- Did the speaker capture the attention of the audience? *Absolutely captured mine. All questions revolved around familiar people, familiar achievements, and familiar stories.*
- Did the speaker establish some connection and rapport with the audience? *70%-90% for me.*
- Did the speaker have the audience thinking, "I like this speaker?" *70%-90% for me.*
- Did the speaker have the audience thinking, "Keep going: don't stop" "tell me more?" *Absolutely—I definitely wanted to know more. I wanted to know where the speaker was going.*
- Did the speaker have the audience thinking, "The speaker is just like me?" *70%-90% for me.*
- Did the speaker constrain the opening between 5–10 % of the time? *Yes—180 words out of a total of 3,100 words = 6%. As far as time goes, opening was 1.25 minutes of a total of 18 minutes = 7%.*

Here is another example of an opening with questions. This is a very famous historic speech delivered on July 5, 1852 by a black man when slavery was legal in the USA.

"What to the Slave is the 4th of July?" presented by Frederick Douglass in 1852

Fellow citizens, pardon me, allow me to ask, why am I called upon to speak here today? What have I, or those I represent, to do with your national independence? Are the great principles of political freedom and of natural justice, embodied in that Declaration of Independence, extended to us? And am I, therefore, called upon to bring our humble offering to the national altar, and to confess the benefits and express devout gratitude for the blessings resulting from your independence to us?

Let's revisit the Steve Jobs Stanford commencement talk.

You are already familiar with this speech. Here is the opening.

I am honored to be with you today for your commencement from one of the finest universities in the world (humility + very brief greeting + acknowledgement of event—commencement + recognition of the university. All in one sentence)

Truth be told, I never graduated from college and this is the closest I've ever gotten to a college graduation (a personal story and humor. In one sentence)

Today I want to tell you three stories from my life. That's it. No big deal. Just three stories (road map characterized by clarity and brevity)

Here is EXERCISE #9 for you. You may have to block out one hour. Select three to five speeches and then analyze how well the opening was crafted. If you have your given speeches or presentations in the past, then do this exercise with your own speeches too. It is a fun and challenging exercise. But the real purpose should be to hammer home the importance of the very good opening.

If you usually open your speeches, especially your important speeches, or speeches at work, or even in your Toastmasters clubs, with the first or second draft, then you are squandering an opportunity to do your best. Creating memorable and attention-grabbing openings takes hard work, knowledge, research, multiple iterations, and a thorough appreciation of the opportunity that is being accorded to you.

Please don't blow it!

Do not constrain your research to speeches only. Look for outstanding openings in documentaries, movies, TV serials, etc. There are jewels of scriptwriting to be found in many places. For example, here is an example of a wonderful opening statement from a TV documentary series: *AMERICA: The Story of Us* that aired on the History Channel.

"We are pioneers and trailblazers. We fight for freedom. We

transform our dreams into the truth. Our struggles become a nation."

This brief but excellent opening clearly meets the speech opening criteria. This same string of four sentences is the opening of each of the 12 episodes covering 400 years of American history. It works magnificently.

Perhaps one of the great keynote challenges in recent times was to follow up after Steve Jobs and his Apple product launch presentations. This challenge fell on Tim Cook. Tim Cook's keynotes open with very creative videos, which subtly capture the spirit (dare I say soul) of what Apple strives to be in this world. In my book, these are magnificent openings—especially, as what follows is (in reality) an informational speech about one or more products.

Check out the opening videos at these links:

Apple Keynote: iPhone 6 & Apple Watch (September 2014 Special Event—HD—CC)

http://www.apple.com/live/2014-sept-event/
https://www.youtube.com/watch?v=OD9ZQ9WylRM
or
Apple Special Event. October 22, 2013
http://www.apple.com/apple-events/october-2013/
https://www.youtube.com/watch?v=4FunXnJQxYU

Almost certainly other corporations will be following this approach in years to come.

Another (statesman/political) speech opening that jumped out at me was the India's prime minister Narendra Modi speaking (in Hindi, not English) in Madison Square Garden New York. I noticed that he achieved very high (if not total) neural resonance in seconds.

https://www.youtube.com/watch?v=tKx3OlHrV9I

He opened with a slogan (*For Mother India?*)—calling for an enthusiastic audience response, (*Victory!*) thereby creating immediate commonality and connection. This took less than 5 seconds. This was followed by a 30-second pause. I repeat a 30-second pause. This is very uncomfortable for beginner speakers, and a fabulous connection enabler for advanced speakers. You can judge by yourself how effective this was. The pause was followed by (in 10 seconds) a reference to everyone living in America as his loving brothers and sisters. In under a minute he had achieved superb neural resonance. It is also worth noting that he concluded the speech using the circular closing technique. He brought back the opening slogan (and audience response), and repeated it thrice. Very effective!

Dear Reader, as far as the techniques and content of speech creation go, I suggest that the chapters on the opening and closing are amongst the most important. It is probably best to start drafting and sketching out your speeches and presentations by focusing initially on the closing and the opening. When reflecting on opening and closing of a speech, the words "primacy" and "recency" are frequently used. Primacy, also called the rule of primacy, or primacy effect, suggests that we remember best what we hear first. The recency rule or the recency effect suggests that we remember and recall best what we hear last. These are conclusions of memory studies, so it makes sense to plan your speech around very strong openings and closings.

If you are a Toastmaster you can download an excellent "Beginning Your Speech" (Digital) resource free. Item: 270DCD

Here is my *tenth wish* for you: May your openings be bold, may they capture your audiences' attention and good will, and may they rapidly generate neural resonance.

Chapter 11

Another Copernican Revolution?

(Rondo 2)

*"Finally we shall place the Sun himself
at the center of the Universe."*
— *Nicolaus Copernicus*

This rondo chapter, like the earlier one, is about the "why" of public speaking.

I have mentioned that there is a wannabe detective inside me. This sleuth keeps wondering, keeps trying to figure out why PS&ST is so effective. Why is the cranial decision making so pliant when exposed to super-speakers and super-storytellers? What is it that makes us tune in to these super-speakers and super-storytellers so readily; when we may well have rejected an identical word-for-word message from a suboptimal speaker? Isn't it uncomfortable to contemplate (especially for the more neurotically rational amongst us, myself included) that our brains are more moved and more persuaded by an effective messenger, than they are by an effective message?

What follows are some ideas that I have been exposed to as a result of my cranial amateur-sleuthing treks.

For centuries it was thought that the earth was at the center of the universe, and that the sun revolved around the earth. Polish astronomer Nicolaus Copernicus is credited with having changed this thinking. His major work, *On the Revolutions of the Celestial Spheres*, published in the 1540s, challenged the long held view that Earth was stationary at the center of the universe with all the planets, the moon and the sun rotating around it. He further argued that the planets circled the sun.

Today we know this is true. Today we know that the earth revolves around the sun. Today this is the way we understand the universe.

While nothing in the universe physically changed in

the 1540s, our understanding of how the universe worked underwent a diametric change. When a similar change in understanding and thinking occurs, it is sometimes referred to as a Copernican Revolution or a Copernican Inversion.

A more recent example of a Copernican Revolution comes to us from the relatively new field of positive psychology. Let's call this a 2nd Copernican Revolution.

Martin Seligman is a founder of positive psychology, a field of study that examines healthy states, such as happiness, etc. In his TED Talk he suggests that we have three different Happy Lives, which are The Pleasant Life, The Engaged Life, and The Meaningful Life. Please plan on watching this TED Talk in due course. (Notice the entertaining and unusual story opening too—captivating!)

Martin Seligman: The new era of positive psychology.
http://www.ted.com/talks/martin_seligman_on_the_
state_of_psychology

The author of the book, *The Happiness Advantage*, Shawn Achor, researches and teaches positive psychology. In this book he argues that we are in the midst of another Copernican Revolution. Our current beliefs, our cultural belief systems say that we should study hard, work hard, achieve success, and this will lead us to happiness. Shawn Achor argues that the world of positive psychology is revealing that we have this diametrically wrong. He argues that it is our ability to get happy first, and stay happy as we study hard, and stay happy as we work hard that leads to success upon success. Happiness here is some combination of The Pleasant Life, The Engaged Life, and The Meaningful Life.

Here is a segment from *The Happiness Advantage*.

Today, a fundamental shift in the field of psychology is underway. For generations we have been led to believe that happiness orbited around success. That if we work hard enough, we will be successful, and only if we are successful will we become happy. Success was thought to be the fixed point of the work universe, with happiness revolving around it. Now thanks to breakthroughs in the burgeoning field of positive psychology, we are learning that the opposite is true. When we are happy—when our mindset and mood are positive—we are smarter, more motivated, and thus more successful. Happiness is at the center and success revolves around it.

Please put this TED Talk on your "to watch" list. Note again: another very effective personal story opening.

Shawn Achor: The happy secret to better work

http://www.ted.com/talks/shawn_achor_the_happy_secret_to_better_work

We have looked at 2 Copernican Inversions. Now, I sometimes feel as if there is a 3rd one going on around us right now.

It is emerging from the vast amount of new knowledge we are learning about our brains. It relates to the way we accept the apparent primacy of rationality, about us being rational beings, about the superiority of the rational mind, and about the undesirability to being emotional when making decisions.

This is a mindset that is ubiquitous and accepted in the professions of engineering and project management. We are expected to think things through to reach the best rational conclusions. And we probably don't think too highly of emotional decision-making.

However, emerging brain knowledge suggests that something diametrically opposite to this may actually be happening.

As our brains evolved over millions of years, they kept growing in size and functionality. The changes have, very simplistically, been categorized into three distinct phases.

First there was the reptilian brain. If we could go back in

time and say hello to all our ancestors, we would eventually discover some of them with no mammalian brain and no new brain—only a reptilian brain: the most ancient part of the brain. All the brainpower of these ancestors was allocated toward survival and reproduction. It has been proposed that this part of the brain generates instinctual behaviors involved in aggression, dominance, and territoriality.

Next to evolve was the mammalian brain, which generates emotions. This is the generator of love, fear, and other emotions.

Most recent to evolve was the new brain, also called the neocortex. This is what separates us from reptiles and other mammals.

Of course we all still have aggression, dominance, territoriality, and emotional responses. Our belief (over the last few centuries) is that these primal emotions and aggressive and territorial behaviors can be, and should be controlled by the rational mind. If this belief were really true, then at a neurobiological level, the neocortex would have ultimate decision-making power and veto power over the reptilian and mammalian brains.

A 3rd Copernican Revolution may eventually conclusively show us that this is not so, that we are only allowed to be rational after having been given permission by the reptilian brain and the mammalian brain.

Let us consider the case of "permissives" from an engineering context to understand this more clearly. The large 2-stroke marine engines that I worked on for so many years have external lubricating oil (LO) pumps and external cooling water (CW) pumps. This means that LO and CW pumps can (actually must) be started before the engine is given permission to start. Once the engine is given a command to start, the control system will perform a check for LO pressure, and only if it is OK, will the control system permit the engine to start.

Similarly, the control system will perform another check on the CW pressure, and only if it is OK, will the control system permit the engine to start.

For a project management analogy, let us consider two tasks, A and B in a project plan. The nature of these tasks is that B can only be started after A is complete. In project management jargon this may be referred to as a "finish-to-start" precedence relationship.

Something similar seems to be happening in our brains. The reptilian brain either controls decision-making, or retains veto power over decision-making. If its reptilian needs for aggression, dominance, and territoriality are met, (LO pressure OK? Yes. CW pressure OK? Yes.) it will permit the mammalian brain to go about its emotional business. If, however, it detects a threat, (LO pressure OK? NO! CW pressure OK? NO!) it is capable of shutting down further processing, and it will allocate energy and resources to attend to the threat at hand. This happens instantly and mainly out of cognition. Attending to the perceived threat means preparing for fight or flight: changes in breathing rates, changes in blood circulation, clenched fists, shallow breathing, etc.

Remember the chapter on the fear of public speaking? Sound familiar?

Assuming that the reptilian brain grants permission to proceed, a similar set of control checks and processing takes place in the mammalian brain. Only when the mammalian brain is satisfied that its emotional needs are met, will it grant permission to the new brain to perform its rational duties.

This description is obviously way too simplistic, but it is the basic argument made by this potential Copernican Revolution. First we are survivors, next we are emotional beings, and lastly (and most recently) we are rational beings.

There may also be some sort of feedback loop activity going

on. All being OK, the reptilian brain allows the mammalian brain to proceed with processing, and once again all being OK, the new brain is allowed to do its work. It may be that after all the brains have done their work, the final decision sign-off is in reverse; i.e. the new brain sends its results to the mammalian brain, and the mammalian brain sends its results to the reptilian brain and the reptilian brain signs-off on the decision. Once this decision is made, then our energy systems are activated and we respond accordingly.

This means that the reptilian brain is the ultimate decider, the mammalian brain is a more powerful influencer, and the new brain is a less powerful influencer.

If this is true, it will require a major re-evaluation of how the hyper-rational worlds of engineering and project management respond, especially when communicating with "deciders."

The unwelcome reality may very well be that the long-held perceived superiority of data and facts while communicating to deciders is really not all that superior.

Let us say that I lead a team of engineers and project managers, and that we have created a marvelous new device that solves a longstanding problem, which is sure to be broadly accepted into the market. Let us assume that you, the reader, also lead a team of engineers and project managers, and that you too have created a slightly less marvelous device which solves the same long-standing problem, and is also sure to be broadly accepted into the market. Let's further assume that my team has decided that we will communicate only with facts and data, confident that this is what really gets our customers to decide, while your team takes advantage of new knowledge and commits to creating a more comprehensive message, targeting all the parts of brains to be receptive to your marketing message.

Keeping the latest understanding from neuroscience in

mind, if I were asked to guess which of our products would be more likely to prevail in the market, I would guess it would be yours.

If the emotional brain (of our potential customer) buys into your product and not into mine, then in all probability you will make the sale.

The argument that decisions are made emotionally (reptilian and mammalian brains) rather than rationally (new brain) is powerfully supported by some stories I read about Antonio Damasio's experience with some of his patients.

Damasio is a trailblazing and award-winning psychologist who is widely respected and admired. He observed that some of his patients seemed incapable of making even simple and basic decisions even though they had full access to the rational part of their brains. Even questions like "When should we have our next appointment?" or "Which restaurant should we go to?" would result in an endless discussion of the pros and cons of each option. These patients would perform just fine on tests for intellectual ability. Their inability to decide even basic things was baffling. Worse, it made these patients non-functional, and resulted in them losing their jobs, experiencing a breakdown of their marriages, etc. It turns out that their brain lesions resulted in a loss of connections between the rational and emotional parts of the brain, and without access to the emotional parts of their brains, they were unable to make decisions.

When I read this, it suddenly made a lot of sense. The rational mind is really a supporting character who has somehow sold us the story that he is the smart one in charge of everything. This may be why so many PM&Es grant so little focus, so little status, and so little importance to PS&ST.

Exposure to this kind of emerging knowledge has helped me get a better sense of why PS&ST is so powerful. They communicate directly with the non-rational parts of our brain and this is where decision-making resides.

It may be that PM&Es (like all of us) have been educated into believing that the new brain is the sun with the reptilian and mammalian brains orbiting around it, controlled by the gravity of the sun.

New knowledge is now pointing to a possibility that much (some say all) of what the new brain believes it has chosen to focus on, think about, and do, is actually plans dictated by the reptilian and mammalian brains. As Nobel prize winning psychologist Daniel Kahneman has wryly noted, *"If this were a movie, the new brain mind would be the supporting character believing itself to be the hero."*

This may explain something I'm guessing we've all intuitively and intellectually experienced: "People cannot be reasoned out of a decision they were never reasoned into—in the first place."

Will a third Copernican revolution require us to **finally place emotions themselves at the center of the decision-making universe, with pure rationality orbiting around and potentially influencing the true deciders**? I am willing to wager that new knowledge will reveal that something along these lines is fundamentally accurate.

Basis this wager, I believe that all of us should recommit ourselves, as often as required, to the acquisition of expertise in PS&ST.

Chapter 12

Storytelling

"Frankly there isn't anyone you couldn't learn
to love, once you've heard their story."
— Quote carried in wallet of children's
television host Mr. Rogers

For those us who default to a strictly intellectual, (sometimes neurotically rational) approach when facing life's challenges and voyages, coming to intelligently acknowledge the sheer power of storytelling is not going to be easy. Nonetheless it is necessary. It took me a long time to rationally acknowledge that storytelling is one of the most powerful ways of persuading. It is one of the most powerful ways of making a meaningful impact in life. Storytelling is one of the most powerful ways to express what we care about in this world. My excuse for this delayed "arrival at correct decision" is a pretty good one actually; I am an engineer. Storytelling was no part of my educational experience. If anything, my training required me to be guarded against stories.

To be fair to those of us with this neurotically rational (OK, if not neurotically rational, at least strictly rational) approach, we were probably educated into it when we were young. It was a theme throughout my educational voyage. An educated and wise person was not to be guided or persuaded by mere emotions, nor be naïve enough to be fooled by stories. The correct and optimal way to make decisions, especially important ones, was to be guided by reasoned argument, facts, and data only.

However, new knowledge always comes along and disrupts some cherished and long-held methodologies. Now new (for me) knowledge requires me to acknowledge and accept the sheer power of storytelling.

The task that I have to accomplish in this chapter is to convince you that storytelling is not the low-status refuge that some of us believe it to be. It is a powerful and necessary component of effective communication. We would do well to excel at it and to understand where its power comes from.

Let me return again to the argument I made in chapters 3 & 7 based around this quotation, *It is harder to decide— really and truly decide—to become a millionaire, than it is to actually become a millionaire.* This time, a modified version of the quotation would be, *It is probably harder to decide—really and truly decide—to commit to becoming an expert storyteller, than it is to actually becoming an expert storyteller.* Again, I am not offering this as an exact science type of statement, but more as a means of recognizing that these are two very different processes.

The first line of Rudyard Kipling's poem "The Ballad of East and West" is *"Oh East is East, and West is West, and never the twain shall meet."* When I was young, growing up in India, I considered this to be basically accurate. Today, however, this kind of thinking is hopelessly outmoded. Look at any engineering team or project team and in all likelihood, the east and the west have met and melded in ways that are admirable and desirable.

I see a similar pattern here. Once it may have been basically accurate to think, "Oh, PS&ST is PS&ST, and PM&E is PM&E, and never the twain shall meet." Well, I predict that they will meet and meld as admirably and desirably as East and West have.

I will now caution the strictly rational reader, that this could be the longest Necessary Bridge you will have to cross while making the PM&E to PS&ST voyage. There is a clash of (cranial) civilizations of sorts going on—and it's best not to underestimate the nature of this clash.

However, other professions are increasingly utilizing storytelling, and so must we. The book *TATA Log: Eight Modern*

Stories from a Timeless Institution by Harish Bhat provides an example. The author has been a successful business leader, (managing director and chief operating officer) of large organizations, and is simultaneously a master storyteller. The storytelling advantage is beautifully articulated in the foreword of the book. *In the world of business, storytelling is not a skill that is particularly envied—the expression has pejorative undertones, and suggests tall tales and fiction rather than fact.* Sounds familiar? *But Harish's kind of storytelling plays a valuable role in business. How do you assemble solid facts and incidents, often mundane when they occurred, into a narrative that interests the reader, and leaves him or her with an overarching message? That is the art of corporate storytelling. Stories and narratives are at the heart of human evolution.*

I hope you are beginning to agree.

Why become an expert storyteller? In one sentence, **Because Stories Make Us Care.** If we care for anything at all in this world, then storytelling is a premium way to express and empower that care. We care deeply about our professions; storytelling is a way of expressing that deep care. A common line in the PS&ST world is "Your audience does not care how much you know, until they know how much you care." This is why opening with a story is so popular. It allows all of us to care, together, about the topic that is to be introduced and discussed. Starting off with high neural resonance is a good thing!

At this point dear reader, I ask that you block out about 1 to 2 hours of uninterrupted time and go through the following TED Talks. Isn't TED one heck-of-a-gift to this world? I ask that you enjoy the talks, and simultaneously view and listen to them as both an expert student, and as a professional determined to acquire expertise in storytelling. Be a detective; capture the clues to this unfamiliar craft.

The first three are wonderful talks celebrating and evangelizing storytelling. They cover stories in drama, business, leadership, change, politics, public relations, and public interest. I request you to also pay particular attention to the slides (visual aids) and compare how different they are to what we PM&Es routinely use and endure. Please also be on a lookout for a theme that will recur whenever you are absorbing storytelling: **Whoever Tells the Best Story Wins.**

Andrew Stanton: The clues to a great story
http://www.ted.com/talks/andrew_stanton_the_clues_
to_a_great_story
TEDxHogeschoolUtrecht—Steve Denning: Leadership storytelling
https://www.youtube.com/watch?v=RipHYzhKCuI
TEDxVancouver — Greg Power: The power of story
https://www.youtube.com/watch?v=iExl_rF7zgQ

From these talks we can pick up the following nuggets:
— The greatest story commandment is "Make me care."
— Storytelling has guidelines, not hard and fast rules.
— Another fundamental thing we learned is about liking your main character.
— A story must have a theme. There should be a grand design under it, despite seeming to depict historical lineage.
— The best stories infuse wonder.
— The fine line between speaking and being heard is storytelling.
— Great stories are powerful and capricious.
— Storytelling is deeply embedded in our DNA.
— All culture is nothing but a series of stories.
— We want our news packaged as drama.

— To work well, stories must be irresistible, believable, and unforgettable.

We now know that:
— Stories are a powerful way to engage an audience.
— It is a great idea to start any speech, talk, or presentation with a story.
— In business, stories should preferably be minimalist.
— Feelings (emotions) drive decisions. (Copernican Revolution 3?)
— Unconscious mind is driven by emotions. (Copernican Revolution 3?)
— Emotions are organized as story narratives.
— Stories are saved directly into memory.
— Emotions lead to action. (Copernican Revolution 3?)
— Stories drive behavior. (Copernican Revolution 3?)
— Emotional narratives stored in memory help us to speak and be heard

Fundamentals of storytelling include:
— There should be an opening, middle, and ending.
— Stories have a conflict and a resolution.
— Stories revolve around a hero or protagonist who overcomes something during the story and is changed by the end of the story.
— The conflict is usually in the form of man-against-man, man-against-obstacles, or man-against-himself.

In PM&E, there is bound to be a (dormant) treasure trove of man-against-obstacles (the laws of physics and science) stories, like in no other profession. Our opportunity is to unearth and tell these stories.

The most basic guideline for story construction is, "Every

sentence in the story must either be developing the characters or moving the action forward."

The next three talks are more formula-based talks: How to create a story.

Dave Lieber TED Talk, "The dog of my nightmares"
https://www.youtube.com/watch?v=Xig_r8eKfeM
Kurt Vonnegut talk, "The shapes of stories"
https://www.youtube.com/watch?v=oP3c1h8v2ZQ&list
=PL991B74289AE23E10
Nancy Duarte TED talk, "The secret structure of great talks"
http://www.ted.com/talks/nancy_duarte_the_secret_
structure_of_great_talks

It is also suggested that you look at the storytelling tips from the experts at Moth:

http://themoth.org/tell-a-story/storytelling-tips

If you have any stories in your current presentations or speeches, this would be a good time to check them out against the suggested formulas or guidelines.

In my experience the biggest issue with PM&E stories is that we tend to include too much technical or other detail, just because we know the material—and believe that it provides necessary context. Most stories work just fine with no technical details at all. As long as each sentence in the story is either developing the characters, or setting the scene, or moving the action forward, or describing the conflict and the outcome, or summarizing the point of the story, the story will be more memorable and therefore repeatable. If the story includes an excellent one-line sound bite, then the story is most likely to be remembered and repeated.

Here are questions associated with storytelling and can be used as a checklist for your stories.

1. Is this really a story, with a proper start-middle-end? *I*

am embarrassed to report that many times I did not get past this question. I was mistaking speeches for stories.

2. Is there a conflict and a resolution?

3. Is there a point to the story? Is the point clearly made?

4. Is there a good sound-bite line? Is the line memorable and repeatable?

5. Does each and every line either develop characters, or set the scene, or move the action forward, or describe the conflict and the outcome, or summarize the point?

6. Go over each and every sentence and ask, "What is the worst thing that would happen if I removed this entire sentence?" *This proved to be a surprisingly effective exercise for me.*

7. Is this story true? This is a tricky one. Better questions may be "Is this story emotionally true?" "Could there be 'lies-by-omission' or 'deception' issues associated with this story?"

8. Are the characters likeable?

9. Will this story make my audience care?

10. Am I the hero of the story? Or is the main point being made by another character in the story? Is the wisdom being provided by someone other than me?

11. Is this story memorable and repeatable?

12. Is there a purpose to telling this story? If the story is a part of a longer speech or presentation, what is the purpose?

So far we have seen some features and characteristics of stories, we have gone over some guidelines on how to create stories, and how to differentiate stories from not-stories, and we have got a checklist against which we can check our own stories.

Now I want to return to some more thoughts on why storytelling is so important and why you should commit to becoming an expert in storytelling.

Sun Tzu is a historical Chinese general who is said to have lived around 500 BC. One of the most famous military treatises of all time is associated with his name. It is called *The Art of War: Sun Tsu*. It is well known in military circles and is part of some advanced leadership and management curriculum. Sun Tzu's wisdom has been passed down for centuries. It is comprised of 13 chapters, each of which is devoted to one aspect of warfare.

Two components of Sun Tzu's approach are:

1. To win a hundred battles is not the height of skill. To subdue the enemy without fighting is. Indeed the History Channel documentary *The Art of War* refers to this *(the best way to win is not to fight at all)* as the ultimate secret.
2. The term "orthodox" refers to "by the book" operations. "Unorthodox" refers to flexible, creative, unexpected maneuvers. The great general must master both the orthodox and the unorthodox. Generals engage according to the orthodox, but victory goes to the master of the unorthodox.

It is possible for me, in my mind's eye, to equate being an effective storyteller to being a general who wins his or her battles-of-day-to-day-life-in-times-of-peace without fighting, or with the least amount of fighting. It is further possible for me to equate storytelling with unorthodox operations and flexible operations; and to predict that in the battles-of-day-to-day-life-in-times-of-peace the generals who excel in the unorthodox skill of storytelling will win. This is especially so when trying to bring about change in stodgy, rigid, and—dare I say—orthodox organizations.

We keep returning to the observation: Whoever tells the best story wins.

A very famous historical example of this can be seen in the movie *Amistad*. A lawyer is tasked with an impossible situation. Try to get justice for a group of slaves who had revolted on a sea voyage—when slavery was legal. An ex-president John Adams tells the lawyer that in his experience, "Whoever tells the best story wins." The lawyer follows this advice and, against all odds and expectations, prevails.

Do you remember the Microsoft and Apple comparison from the preface?

Two dominant companies, Microsoft and Apple, drove the PC revolution. Microsoft initially focused on providing really useful and ubiquitous products, but was (in my opinion) not too concerned about design. Apple was (in my opinion) deeply concerned about design. Its stunning success with its beautifully designed products eventually brought about a paradigm shift. Great design brought very real advantages. I am arguing that skillful storytelling has many parallels to great design. I am of the opinion that Apple understood the power of storytelling better than Microsoft did, and used it to great advantage.

Once we look at storytelling seriously, it is difficult to avoid these conclusions.

1. Whoever tells the best story wins.
2. Stories make us care.
3. Regardless of intellectual prowess and advantage, nobody cares about what we know, until they know how much we care.
4. The really important issues of this world are ultimately decided by the story that grabs the most attention and is repeated most often.
5. Stories capture attention much more efficiently than facts.
6. When we control attention, we control conclusions.

7. Stories stick; facts are forgotten.
8. Facts tell; stories sell.
9. Presidential elections can be won and lost on storytelling. Here it is again: Whoever tells the best story wins.
10. Politics is fundamentally about story.

This is a formidable list to fight against.

I strongly urge you to act on your commitment to storytelling soonest by procuring some books and products on storytelling. I strongly urge you to block out some time in the weeks and months ahead to learn more about storytelling.

Here are some of my recommendations.

Book 1

Whoever Tells the Best Story Wins: How to Use Your Own Stories to Communicate With Power and Impact by Annette Simmons. (Kindle Version US $10)

This book is simple, compelling, and has many useful and practical story-capturing exercises. It is an easy and essential read. I heard this author present at a PMI-H event and she made a compelling case. She was mesmerizing when she shared her veterans' affairs consulting story where she used story and poetry to get the result she wanted. One of her other books, *The Story Factor*, has been named one of "The best 100 business books of all time." So she is a recognized expert in this field.

Book 2

The Leader's Guide to Storytelling: Mastering the Art & Discipline of Business Narrative by Steven Denning. (Kindle Version US $16)

The author has had a very distinguished career and a strictly rational background like ours. The book also provides some very nice templates for crafting the many different types of stories that can benefit any business.

Book 3

Strategic Storytelling: How to Create Persuasive Business Presentations by Dave McKinsey (Kindle version US $3)

A very analytical approach with very detailed explanation of best practices of business slides.

Product 1

Edge of Their Seats Storytelling Home Study Course for Speakers: How to Keep Your Audiences Riveted, Revved Up and Ready for Your Message—Craig Valentine.

I have attended some keynotes and breakout sessions of Craig Valentine and loved this 6 CD set. I whole-heartedly recommend it to anyone who wishes to acquire expertise in storytelling. This will be one of the very few products I recommend. Cost US $300.

I'll close this chapter with a personal story I told at a local Moth event. The theme of the event was "Altered." We had to tell a personal story of when and how we were altered. Notice how different the writing style has to be. Check it out against the storytelling guidelines. This is written in a minimalist style, with very little detail, yet retaining emotional truth, and teaching the lesson that fighting is suboptimal. As this was written for Moth, there is no title for the story, but if I had to provide a title it would be either "A Book and a Boss" or "Fixing Is Better than Fighting."

Actually, it is two stories—one nested in another. One story is about the Cuban missile crisis and the other is something that happened to me a long time ago. Both stories teach the same lesson—that fighting is not an optimal option.

Since this is a story more than a speech my speaking rate

is much faster. The target time was five minutes plus or minus one minute.

My speaking rate here is about 150 words per minute, i.e. 50% faster than my preferred speech speaking rate.

Even before I started crafting this story, I knew that someday I would end one of my stories with Kennedy's famous words. Consequently, I started out constructing this story with a very clear end in mind.

Recently I was reading a book called "To Move the World: JFKs Quest for Peace." The very first sentence.

The President of the United States, John F. Kennedy exclaimed in frustration "There's always some son-of-a-bitch who doesn't get the word."

My mind went back to a boss and an incident from over a decade ago.

I was a manager for a ship repair company. My boss … came to me with a fax.

Rashid, Norwegian customer, seismic vessel, lots of work, you're in charge.

I called the Norwegian customer.

He asked: Rashid, can you take care of

engine repairs … yes

steel work … yes

electric work … yes

He continued, "Can you organize a large crane?"

I responded, "Yes, but all this is going to cost you tens of thousand of dollars" (1 minute/ 133/ 133)

He said "I know—proceed."

I arranged everything and called the agent to inform him my team would be attending. Now the agent is the person who looks after all local matters for the ship owner. He told me that the ship would be docking in Galveston dock No. x.

I got my team on dock No. x before the seismic vessel pulled in and was preparing to mobilize, when I saw a fabulous new bright red sports car.

This was unusual. Usually the dockside is full of pickup trucks and old cars.

The guy inside was looking around and getting increasingly angry. He stepped out, looked over my team at the crane and trucks, and seemed to get more angry ... walked off ... and started talking to someone on his cell.

By the time he put the phone down ... he was really angry ... and then he came our way.

"Who's in charge of this crew?" He yelled. (2 minutes / 161/294)

Trying to stay calm and look confident I said, "Me."

"What the bleep are you doing on my dock?"

"Your dock? I'm sorry ... isn't this a public dock? ... sorry. I did not know."

"Yes, I've leased this dock" ... "I've paid tens of thousands of dollars for it" ... "There's always some SOB who doesn't get the word." ... "Take your crew and leave ... get off my dock!"

Here, I had just spent tens of thousands of dollars. And I had been very publically yelled at in front of all my crew.

How could I have known otherwise? Neither the Norwegian owner nor the local agent said anything about going to a private berth.

I got in touch with the Norwegian customer, who was also at the dock. Gave him a brief update.

He went and spoke to the angry man. He fared no better than me. (3 minutes/ 148/442)

I really felt for him. Suddenly all his planning was for naught. He certainly had bigger problems than me now. He agreed to cover all my costs.

My team and yours truly ignominiously left the dock ... evicted!

Next day ... back at the office ... boss called me "Rashid, You're in charge of the office today."

"Where you going, boss? What about the other bosses?"

"Oh, they are all coming with me. We are going to Galveston."

I did not know whether to feel glad or sad that I was not going to be present to see some fighting and fireworks. I would have gladly contributed my share of fireworks ... after all, I had just been very publically humiliated.

Next day back at the office, I asked, "Boss, how did it go? Did you'll have a good fight? Who won?"

"Oh it was nothing. I fixed everything. I just had to un-ruffle some feathers. We are all friends now. No point in fighting." (4 minutes/ 163/ 605)

And I don't really know whether he said this ... but I heard it. "Fixing is better than fighting."

Fixing is better than fighting. Fixing is harder than fighting.

I had decided, a long time ago, to be a better fixer than a fighter.

My mind returned to the book I was reading. Here was a fight on a terrifying global scale.

JFK had just uttered history's most famous SOB statement.

The USA and the USSR were on the brink of nuclear war.

Two combatants-in-chief, Kennedy and Khrushchev, were looking squarely at a planet-annihilating blunder.

By dumb luck our planet survived.

After the crisis passed, both men ... profoundly altered, said ... "ENOUGH"! They launched peace initiatives.

Both leaders made a necessary transition from fighting to fixing. (5 minutes/ 125/ 730)

JFK put it this way.

"So let us not be blind to our differences, but let us also direct attention to our common interests ... for in the final analysis ... we all share this small planet ... we all breathe the same air ...

we all cherish our children's future ... and we are all mortal."
   Good enough for a boss and for JFK: Good enough for me.
(5.5 minutes/69/799)

Dear Reader, I remind you that transitioning from "strictly rational professional" to "storytelling expert" can be fairly difficult. It may initially have to be a leap of faith, but you will come to discover its power eventually. I know I struggled with it. Indeed If I had not heard Annette Simmons speak at the PMI-H event, and subsequently bought her book, I would have taken even longer to commit to acquiring storytelling expertise.

If you have truly committed to become a PS&ST expert, have committed time and money on a project plan toward this goal, then I urge you, and urge you again to immediately procure the two books and one product I have recommended. Now is the time to act. Indeed, create a parallel project task in your plan to work on storytelling on a continuous basis. Good luck!

Chapter 13

Orthodox Public Speaking and Storytelling Competencies

I believe that to become an expert (and subsequently victorious) PS&ST we have to master a combination of orthodox and unorthodox knowledge sets, and be willing and able to use them skillfully so that we may be victorious, or at least not defeated, in the arena of effective communications.

In earlier chapters we have covered the basic parts of a speech, and have stressed that the closing and openings are disproportionately important—due to the fact that memory retention is strongly biased toward primacy and recency.

Other important components of PS&ST that contribute to a speech, presentation, or storytelling being more memorable are humor, vocal variety, facial expressions, body language, gestures, stage usage, acting, etc. I have divided the range of skills that contribute to effective PS&ST into two categories, orthodox and unorthodox. The orthodox ones are far more accepted and easy to achieve than the unorthodox ones.

Orthodox skills, for me at least, include humor, vocal variety, gestures, body language, facial expressions, staging, acting, etc.

I tend to think of connection with audience, listening deeply to your audience, drawing in the energy and good will of your audience, the ability to go into flow while speaking, all as unorthodox competencies, because they are less common and more difficult to achieve.

As unorthodox skills become more and more utilized, they tend to move into the orthodox column and the search for the new unorthodox continues. This is the search for new knowledge, new meaning, creativity, and connecting old ideas in new ways. The search for the unorthodox in PS&ST (as in PM&E) is where our innovation in PS&ST (and PM&E) lies.

I described storytelling as unorthodox in the last chapter, but given the fact that it is so widely being recognized as an unparalleled force in public speaking, it is only a matter of time when it will come to be seen as an orthodox competency, i.e. we will all simply have to include storytelling any time we are presenting, as surely as we include vocal variety and gestures, etc.

During my transition from "strictly rational" to "PS&ST aficionado," I learned that effective communication is much, much more than just the words. But even I was surprised to grudgingly discover how little the words alone mattered. It was a sobering discovery, but when new knowledge and personal experience disrupt cherished beliefs, then it is time for me to accept and embrace the new approaches too.

Here are some stories, documentaries, and incidents that made me accept that there are much more than words and strict rationality to consider on the road to PS&ST expertise.

The 1960 Presidential Debates

John F. Kennedy and Richard M. Nixon contested the first US presidential debates. The legacy of these debates is both strange and revealing—especially to those amongst us who remain stubbornly convinced that it is the words, the logic, and the rational elements of a speech that matter most. I do not want to suggest that strong logical and rational arguments do not count; they are necessary, but only as a part of an effective package.

Please consider taking a look at this video now and reading the article that follows it.

http://www.history.com/topics/us-presidents/kennedy-nixon-debates

There were two audiences for these debates, one that watched on television and another that listened to the radio. Some background: *The U.S. presidential election of 1960 came at a decisive time in American history. Internationally, there was a heated Cold War, alongside a revolutionary regime in Cuba. On the domestic front, there was a struggle for civil rights and desegregation.*

At a time when the need for strong leadership was all too obvious, two vastly different candidates vied for the presidency: John F. Kennedy, a young but dynamic Massachusetts senator from a powerful New England family, and Richard Nixon, a seasoned lawmaker who was currently serving as vice president.

With little more than a single unremarkable term in the U.S. senate under his belt, the 43-year-old Kennedy lacked Nixon's extensive foreign policy experience and had the disadvantage of being one of the first Catholics to run for president on a major party ticket. Nixon, by contrast, had spent nearly eight years as the country's second-in-command after an illustrious career in Congress during which he cast crucial votes on domestic and international issues–all by the age of 39.

Nixon has the opening advantage. *During the debates: Each held forth skillfully and presented remarkably similar agendas. Both emphasized national security, the threat of communism, the need to strengthen the U.S. military and the importance of building a brighter future for America.*

Yet after the debates: *While most radio listeners called the first debate a draw or pronounced Nixon the victor, the senator from Massachusetts won over the 70 million television viewers by a broad margin.*

Two years after the Kennedy-Nixon debates, Nixon, the man on the losing end acknowledged his fatal misstep in his memoir "Six Crises": "I should have remembered that 'a picture is worth a thousand words.'"

This story strongly convinced me that when PS&ST, I would do well indeed not to make the same mistake that

Richard Nixon made. I would do well to pay attention to vocal variety, gestures, body language, facial expressions, etc. They communicate a lot more than I assumed they did.

I was even more strongly convinced about the great necessity of planning a speech well beyond the words, after watching the documentary *"History Channel: Secrets of Body Language."* I ask that you block out about 90 minutes and study this documentary diligently. After watching this documentary a few times there was no serious doubt left in my mind that body language, facial expressions, vocal variety, and gestures are undisputedly game-changers in the world of communication. They are the sticky and memorable parts of the message. These, more than script and words, are what bring victory to campaigning politicians. It is a sobering thought indeed. But if it is indeed true, then I ignore this knowledge at my own peril.

In this documentary (1 hour 14 minutes) Patti Wood, body language expert, describes US President Barack Obama's skill at vocal variety like this: *It's so powerful. Because what it does, is … it doesn't really matter what he's saying … because his voice tells you what you should be feeling about what he's saying … the words become irrelevant. You might not even remember the word message after he's finished speaking … but boy did you feel something really, really powerful.*

Let's read this again. "It doesn't really matter what he's saying." Really? Now read this. "The words become irrelevant. You might not even remember the word message after he's finished." Don't remember the word message? Really?

After acknowledging this (for me) new knowledge—words do not matter that much—a paradigm shift for me took place, and I began to deliberately plan these parts of my speech delivery and specifically sought feedback from audience members with requests like this.

"Please give me your honest feedback on my vocal variety, my gestures, my facial expressions, etc."

"Was my movement on stage clear? Did it appear pointless, like I was pacing? Was my movement confusing?"

Requesting this sort of specific feedback is more valuable than I can express. It has to become part of any good learning plan. The feedback I get is usually something like this.

"Your vocal variety was usually good Rashid, but occasionally you slipped into either 'monotone' or 'sameness' and you lost my attention. I had to struggle to focus. Sometimes you spoke too softly and I had to struggle to hear you."

"Your gestures are generally effective and natural Rashid, but sometimes you use one hand much more than the other, especially if you are holding a presentation-controlling device. This becomes a distraction."

"Your stage movement is not really effective and you should work more on it, Rashid. There is nothing specifically wrong with it, but it is not as good as the rest of your presentation. Sometime you move back unconsciously, and this can make the audience feel you are disconnecting from them. You do not utilize the stage area as well as you should."

"Your facial expressions could do with some work. Be a little less inhibited with your facial expressions. Expand the range of your facial expressions."

This is all fantastic feedback. Absorbing feedback like a sponge is a sure accelerant toward the acquisition of expertise.

I am going to point you to what I believe are orthodox PS&ST competencies, make a few key observations, and point you to some resources to consider.

Vocal Variety

Beautifully scripted words, delivered without vocal variety, will be ineffective and likely forgotten. This is a fact. Simple words and simple sentences, even if grammatically or otherwise incorrect, delivered with outstanding vocal variety (passion) will be far more effective and memorable.

This is a relatively simple skill to acquire. It does need practice, a willingness to be uncomfortable, even embarrassed. The return on investment is high.

When listening to the news, or a speech, try speaking along with the broadcaster or speaker and listen for the difference in your vocal variety. This is EXERCISE #10. The same exercise can be done with songs too—just speak instead of singing. This simple exercise can be practiced at any time. It opened my eyes to how poor my vocal variety initially was.

If you have joined Toastmasters, there is a very nice downloadable document called "Your Speaking Voice" that is available free to all Toastmasters.

http://www.toastmasters.org/199-YourSpeakingVoice

I now consider vocal variety to be such an important skill, that if you can afford it, I recommend that you go to a voice training coach as early as possible on your PS&ST voyage.

Gestures, Body Language, Facial Expressions, and Acting

When watching famous speeches, occasionally shut off the sound and pay attention to gestures, stage movement, and body language. This is your EXERCISE #11. Then compare these to a video recording of one of your presentations. The pros make it look really easy and natural. Don't let them fool you for a second; they have had a lot of feedback and coaching. They have made the necessary time and money commitments.

For example, even though John F. Kennedy had been in Congress for 12 years and was a renowned speaker, he still hired a coach when campaigning for the presidency. His biographer Richard Reeves said in Jeffrey Sachs's book, *To Move the World: JFK's Quest for Peace*, of Kennedy's practice sessions: *"Home alone in Washington, he would put on a silk bathrobe, pour himself a brandy, light up a cigar, and speak along with records of Winston Churchill's greatest speeches."*

This is the road to acquiring expertise all over again—constant practice and expert coaching/feedback. This lines up squarely with the observation that the expert on experts Anders Ericsson has repeatedly made.

If you have joined Toastmasters, "Gestures: Your Body Speaks" is available free to you.

http://www.toastmasters.org/201-Gestures

I also recommend a book called *"The Pin Drop Principle: Captivate, Influence and Communicate Better Using the Time-Tested Methods of Professional Performers"* by David Lewis and G. Riley Mills.

A comment about acting: I initially felt the same way about acting as I did about storytelling—and once again I have to accept that I was wrong. The principles and techniques used by professional actors are powerful communication tools and there is no good reason why all of us should not study and use them.

Here is the HBR article on expertise from chapter 6 saying the same thing: *Working with a drama school, the authors created a set of acting exercise for managers that remarkably enhanced executives' powers of charm and persuasion.*

Once again, if you can afford it, I recommend that you sign up with a drama coach or take some acting classes as early as practical on your PS&ST voyage. You will be a better communicator and a better PS&ST for it.

Humor

Humor is not easy in PS&ST. Even folks who can easily make others laugh when conversing, or when hosting an event, struggle with humor in PS&ST. So if you fall into this group, you have plenty of company. Don't let this stop you. Humor in PS&ST is a skill that is absolutely worth having. So commit to working toward this.

A common mistake is to include jokes or funny incidents that do not relate to the topic at hand. Humor should only be used when it is relevant to the message being delivered. There is almost always potential for humor in any situation. Laughter relaxes an audience, and humor releases tension. Memory is significantly enhanced in this state, so uncovering or revealing the humorous side of the situation is the goal. Gentle self-deprecating humor is always a good idea, but ensure that you do not inadvertently compromise your professional credibility in the process. The audience must continue to view you as an expert or authority on the subject you are speaking about. It is a balancing act that you as a speaker must constantly be mindful of.

If you are a Toastmaster, and have completed the Competent Communicator manual, consider getting two advanced manuals for humorous and entertaining speech project practice. "The Entertaining Speaker" (Item 226A). "Humorously Speaking" (Item 226O)

Here are some resource recommendations to take your humor incorporating skills to the next level:

Stand-Up Comedy: The Book by Judy Carter.

"Laff Pack" by Darren LaCroix. This is a nice and reasonably priced assortment of audio lessons, DVDs and a book.

In this chapter, more than any other, I will be asking this of you, my customer: Please seek outside resources to acquire expertise in these orthodox competencies. There are thousands of alternate resources, and I recommend you investigate some of those too before finalizing your procurement decision. Good luck on your journey to mastering these orthodox competencies. Without these skills in place, acquired through study, practice, and feedback, you will probably not rise above average. And if you do not seek honest feedback, you may never even recognize this as mediocrity.

We have come far enough on this PS&ST voyage that you may be having a sense in which direction you would like to further develop it. Take some time to reflect on where you would like to take your PS&ST competence after you complete your current project.

Perhaps you want to continue to rise within an organizational structure—always comfortable, capable, and confident of speaking superbly in any situation, whether it be with investors, bosses, colleagues, teams, vendors, contractors, or customers.

If this is the case I am going to recommend that you consider purchasing one or more of these books:

10 Simple Secrets of the World's Greatest Business Communicators by Carmine Gallo

Pitch Perfect: How to Say It Right the First Time, Every Time by Bill McGowan and Alisa Bowman

Speaker, Leader, Champion: Succeed at Work Through the Power of Public Speaking by Jeremy Donovan and Ryan Avery

The Presentation Secrets of Steve Jobs: How to Be Insanely Great in Front of Any Audience by Carmine Gallo

Perhaps you have come to enjoy the camaraderie and experience of being with others who inhabit your PS&ST world. You may someday want to try your hand at dramatics or some other performance art. If you feel this may be a future calling, I recommend you procure the earlier mentioned book:

The Pin Drop Principle: Captivate, Influence and Communicate Better Using the Time-Tested Methods of Professional Performers by David Lewis and G. Riley Mills.

Perhaps you may sense that in the future you will be called to public service or politics. Here are three recommendations:

Lend Me Your Ears: All You Need To Know About Making Speeches and Presentations by Max Atkinson

Speak Like Churchill, Stand Like Lincoln: 21 Powerful Secrets of History's Greatest Speakers by James C. Hume

Say It Like Obama and WIN: The Power of Speaking With Purpose and Vision by Shel Leanne

Perhaps you may want to speak at TED or participate on a competitive stage. Here are some recommendations:

How to Deliver a TED Talk: Secrets of the World's Most Inspiring Presentations by Jeremy Donovan

Talk Like TED: The 9 Public-Speaking Secrets of the World's Top Minds by Carmine Gallo

How To Win the Toastmasters World Championship of Public Speaking: 2012 International Speech Contest by Jeremy Donovan

Finally, you may someday see yourself expanding, perhaps part-time, into the world of paid professional speaking. If you sense this is a possibility consider procuring this book:

World Class Speaking in Action: 50 Certified World Class Coaches Show You How to Present, Persuade, and Profit by Craig Valentine and Mitch Meyer

Wherever the future takes you, my request to you and my hope of you remains the same: I hope you will take it on yourself to evangelize PS&ST to PM&Es, especially to younger students and professionals so they can be outstanding ambassadors of our professions. Thank you!

Chapter 14

Creating the Icebreaker Speech

*"Courage: Tell the story of who you
are with your whole heart."*
— *Brené Brown, The Power of Vulnerability, TED Talk*

The icebreaker speech may be the most important speech you ever write. Take all the necessary time and do it right. Even if it is not the most important speech you ever give, treat it like it is, especially when crafting it.

Plan, even promise yourself, to invest no less than 1hour of preparation time for every 1 minute of speaking. Good enough for Winston Churchill, good enough for us. The icebreaker we will work on in this chapter should be between four to six minutes. No more.

While the whole world is hardly dying to hear your or my life story, it may be worthwhile to think of this speech as important in the same way that the song "Happy Birthday" is important. I understand that "Happy Birthday" is the most sung (English language) song of all time. In some similar way, you will probably be using one segment or another from your icebreaker speech more frequently than any other speech segment you ever write. Get it right!

Someone is always inquiring about you—wanting to know you, or more about you, or what you do. Be prepared to respond eloquently and authentically. The most effective way to be convincing, persuading, or inspiring, is to tell a relevant personal story just before or after making your point.

Now, without trying to sound preachy or philosophical, let's deal with this thought. "To be eloquent on stage, we must first be eloquent off stage." I heard this approach on a Glenna Salsbury CD and I knew I would never forget it. Her exact line, when speaking to a group of professional speakers was, *"I really believe that we are not eloquent from the platform if we are not eloquent in the grocery store."* She nailed it! Glenna Salsbury is a very famous speaker and a legend in National Speakers Association circles. A variation on this theme could well be "Speak as eloquently to the front desk and administrative staff as you would with those who are interviewing you." Put differently, one way to have good icebreaker speech material is to start out by being a good person (whatever that means to you) to base the speech on. Without being eloquent, graceful, decent, etc., in real life, and off-stage, you may not be able to give an authentic, eloquent, graceful and decent, etc., icebreaker speech on stage. Enough said!

Work hard on preparing a very good, thorough, and concise icebreaker speech.

Parts of the icebreaker can be included in almost any subsequent speech to great effect. A lot of public speaking is about telling stories to make points—and personal stories work best. These personal stories can be extracted from your story files, your failure files, your written (long version) life story, and your icebreaker speech. Efforts put in now will yield speech material long into the future.

An example can be seen in Barack Obama's 2004 Democratic National Convention speech. Many people opine that this is the speech that launched the Obama presidency. The interweaving of his story with the American story and his political message is masterful.

Barack Obama: 2004 Democratic National Convention Keynote Address

http://www.americanrhetoric.com/speeches/convention 2004/barackobama2004dnc.htm

Here is the opening of the speech. Look specifically for the icebreaker elements and see how effectively they have been woven into the fabric of his larger talk.

On behalf of the great state of Illinois, crossroads of a nation, Land of Lincoln, let me express my deepest gratitude for the

privilege of addressing this convention.

Tonight is a particular honor for me because ... Let's face it: My presence on this stage is pretty unlikely. My father was a foreign student, born and raised in a small village in Kenya. He grew up herding goats, went to school in a tin-roof shack. His father—my grandfather—was a cook, a domestic servant to the British.

But my grandfather had larger dreams for his son. Through hard work and perseverance my father got a scholarship to study in a magical place, America, that shone as a beacon of freedom and opportunity to so many who had come before.

While studying here, my father met my mother.

She was born in a town on the other side of the world, in Kansas. Her father worked on oil rigs and farms through most of the Depression. The day after Pearl Harbor my grandfather signed up for duty; joined Patton's army, marched across Europe. Back home, my grandmother raised a baby and went to work on a bomber assembly line. After the war, they studied on the G.I. Bill, bought a house through F.H.A., and later moved west all the way to Hawaii in search of opportunity.

And they, too, had big dreams for their daughter. A common dream, born of two continents.

My parents shared not only an improbable love, they shared an abiding faith in the possibilities of this nation. They would give me an African name, Barack, or "blessed," believing that in a tolerant America your name is no barrier to success. They imagined—They imagined me going to the best schools in the land, even though they weren't rich, because in a generous America you don't have to be rich to achieve your potential.

They're both passed away now. And yet, I know that on this night they look down on me with great pride.

They stand here—And I stand here today, grateful for the diversity of my heritage, aware that my parents' dreams live on in my two precious daughters. I stand here knowing that my story is part of the larger American story, that I owe a debt to all of those who came before me, and that, in no other country on Earth, is my story even possible.

Later in the speech, toward the end, as he is tying it all together, he makes another (self-deprecating) reference to himself, as a skinny kid with a funny name, and it is effective.

I'm not talking about blind optimism here—the almost willful ignorance that thinks unemployment will go away if we just don't think about it, or the health care crisis will solve itself if we just ignore it. That's not what I'm talking about. I'm talking about something more substantial. It's the hope of slaves sitting around a fire singing freedom songs; the hope of immigrants setting out for distant shores; the hope of a young naval lieutenant bravely patrolling the Mekong Delta; the hope of a millworker's son who dares to defy the odds; the hope of a skinny kid with a funny name who believes that America has a place for him, too.

For further analysis of the speech, check out this link.

The Speech That Made Obama President: Analysis and commentary about the speech from THNKR.

https://www.youtube.com/watch?v=OFPwDe22CoY

Work hard on preparing a very good, thorough, and concise icebreaker speech.

Recently, I read a superb book called *The Alliance: Managing Talent in the Networked Age* by Reid Hoffman, Ben Casnocha & Chris Yeh. More than anything I have recently read, this book best predicts the future nature of the employer and employee relationship. Direct from this book: *Here is a principle that Brad Smith applies at Intuit: "We begin every interview by saying, 'Tell me in three to five minutes your life's journey and how it led you to be the person that you are today ... touching on major moments in your life that define who you are and your approach to business and leadership, such as dealing with adverse experiences like a bully, the death of a loved one, or major decisions that went wrong."*

Clearly, these kinds of conversations and questions are going to be increasingly utilized in job interviews, team-building exercises, know-your-new-colleagues exercises, etc.

Here is an example of a very effective personal story. Patricia Fripp, the famous speech coach, frequently tells the story of the advice her father gave her when she was starting out in business, *"Don't concentrate on making a lot of money. Rather, concentrate on becoming the type of person others want to do business with. And most likely you will make a lot of money."* As in the case of the Glenna Salsbury "eloquent" quote, I knew I would never forget this line. She is able to include stories like this in many of her talks and products; they are super-effective.

Aim to capture something similar from your life for your icebreaker, which can subsequently be used for interviews too.

Having your life story written down in no less than five thousand words, followed by a six- to seven-hundred word icebreaker speech provides excellent preparation and practice for the future Brad Smith/Intuit type questions and conversations that will inevitably come your way.

Returning now to our icebreaker speech. The first rule: be authentic.

Once again we have to come back to "know yourself." Doing the necessary "know yourself" exercises prior to writing this speech is just plain smart. I reiterate; do not do a great disservice to your audience, even disrespect your audience, by not being authentic ... by not knowing yourself. You do not have the right! Let me one more time remind you to do some type of "know yourself", "know your values" exercise **in**

writing. It will be well worth your time.

Here are three suggestions. I found the book *The Great Work of Your Life: A Guide for the Journey to Your True Calling* by Stephen Cope to be incredible. I suggest you get this or a similar book and read it, taking the necessary time. It is also a great example of the power of storytelling.

Some years ago I did the exercises in the book KEEP YOUR EYES ON THE PRIZE: *An Exercise in Life Purpose, Random Acts of Kindness and Generosity* by Frederick Pearce and Angela Christensen. A disclosure: Frederick is a friend, a Toastmaster in one of my clubs, and I have done some coaching with him. This book is short, full of practical exercises, and can be completed fairly quickly. If you do these exercises sincerely and thoroughly, you will end up with a life purpose statement, a mission statement, an icon, and a motto. With these statements, you will have some core material for your icebreaker speech already in place.

The third book recommendation to complete at some time, preferably before the icebreaker is *The Values Factor: The Secret to Creating an Inspired and Fulfilling Life* by Dr. John Demartini. In my opinion, John Demartini is an extraordinary trailblazer.

And, I might as well get this out of the way—right away. Don't brag, show off, or similar. No one, including you, enjoys listening to a braggart. Just plan on sharing yourself, flaws and failures included. Save the heroic details of your "I Climbed Everest" or "I Conquered Adversity" or "I Built an Empire" or "I'm the Best in the World" adventures for another speech. If you must, touch on these (no more than a sentence or two) in your icebreaker. I am not being unkind here, simply suggesting that these details belong to another speech. If you have achieved the extraordinary, (Everest, Adversity, Empire, Gold Medal) please accept my sincere and hearty congratulations. And pass them on to all those who supported you too. You have great speech material to draw on. You will shine.

Whether we are trying to persuade our spouses, (be reasonable; do everything my way—honey), or our children (more fresh vegetables, less processed food—sweethearts), or our colleagues (my approach is clearly better than yours—colleague) or our bosses (more money please, preferably right away—boss), or our direct reports (come on folk, let's get it done—team) we are pitching.

I have watched less effective communicators, some in senior leadership positions, who loathe pitching, and take weeks or months to convince others, especially about change, while great communicators get it done first-time-right and move on. Wow, what an advantage.

I recall this short exercise from one of my Craig Valentine CD products. First Craig says, "If you are in speaking, you are in sales." The engineer in me struggled with this for a long time but he is right. Resistance is futile, not to mention career-retarding. If that is not enough, he has the listener repeat after him, using your own name. This is EXERCISE #12.

Remind yourself that you are speaking or presenting with a purpose. In my case, I had to say out loud and then repeat, "I, Rashid N. Kapadia, am in speaking, therefore I, Rashid N. Kapadia, am in sales. I, Rashid N. Kapadia, am in speaking, therefore I, Rashid N. Kapadia am in sales." Fortunately, I got it.

Variations of this exercise could be, "I, Rashid N. Kapadia, am presenting, therefore I, Rashid N. Kapadia, am persuading", or "I, Rashid N. Kapadia, am communicating, therefore I, Rashid N. Kapadia, am campaigning." Saying this repeatedly, and out loud, helps make the transition easier.

I've been speaking to you and selling this to you, "Use your icebreaker speech to tell your story with your whole heart, authentically and engagingly."

I'm presenting to you and persuading you to, "Use your icebreaker speech to tell your story with your whole heart, authentically and engagingly."

I'm communicating with you and campaigning for you to, "Use your icebreaker speech to tell your story with your whole heart, authentically and engagingly."

I am pitching for you to, "Use your icebreaker speech to tell your story with your whole heart, authentically and engagingly."

Returning again to our icebreaker speech preparation, let's begin specific planning. It may be worthwhile for you to do your icebreaker speech in parallel with mine. This is EXERCISE #13. Convert your written life story into an Icebreaker speech.

From chapter 8 "Ending Your Speech," after you have committed to a speech, get these basic questions answered:

What is the topic? *An icebreaker speech.*

What am I going to speak about? *Myself—using guidelines from the Toastmasters Icebreaker project. "I will introduce myself, and give some information about my background, interests, and ambitions."*

What has my boss/customer/supplier/event planner asked me to speak about? *Not Applicable.*

Next come the more important questions.

What do I want my audience to be feeling at the very end? *We are all the same. We are in this together. We have a shared destination. We can work together.*

I want to be guided by, and loosely base my closing on the conclusion of Sting's TED Talk.

Sting: "How I started writing songs again"

http://www.ted.com/talks/sting_how_i_started_writing_songs_again

Here is Sting's ending. *And so here I am at TED, I suppose to tell that story, and I think it's appropriate to say the obvious that there's a symbiotic and intrinsic link between storytelling and community, between community and art, between community and science and technology, between community and economics. It's my belief that abstract economic theory that denies the needs of community or denies the contribution that community makes to economy is shortsighted, cruel, and untenable.*

The fact is, whether you're a rock star or whether you're a welder in a shipyard, or a tribesman in the upper Amazon, or the queen of England, at the end of the day, we are all in the same boat.

I remember a very specific feeling when listening to the end of this talk and that is the same emotion I would like to leave my audience with. If you read my life story you will recall that I spent four years as a marine engineering apprentice in a shipyard; and this talk evoked very strong memories for me.

What do I want my audience to remember of this speech? *My story. Acknowledge and remember that (1) I truly shared myself, and (2) here is someone who has reached out to me and wants to work with me.*

What do I want my audience to commit to after this speech? *Commit to getting to know me better. Commit to the idea "we are on the same side" and that there is no reason why we cannot work together.*

What perspective of my audience do I want to change after this speech? *If they felt "he's not like me" or "he's different from me" or "we've nothing in common," I would like that perspective to be changed.*

What is my call to action? *That we commit to wishing each other well.*

Tentatively, this will be a draft of closing of my icebreaker. I am assuming this icebreaker will be given to a (1) Toastmasters club I have newly joined, or (2) some type of community event or (3) some kind of corporate "team building/get to know your new colleagues" gathering, where we are asked to introduce ourselves over four to six minutes. I would modify it for a more formal or corporate situation. Additionally I would memorize this thoroughly.

A maritime tradition, dating back thousands of years, calls for a ceremonial blessing when a newly built ship is launched from slipway to sea, "May God Bless Her and All Who Sail in Her."

Now, as I begin yet another new voyage, may I shamelessly ask you for a gift. A gift that will cost you neither time nor treasure. I ask for your good wishes. More than anything else, I seek your good wishes. And if these should be granted easily, and generously, then may I ask for more, may I ask for your blessings.

I know in a way that is non-negotiable, that all of us, whether we are speakers on a stage, or slum dwellers in squalor, or even if we are sovereigns of state, one way or another, we are all in the same boat; together.

And one way or another, now and always, my wish for each and every one of you, indeed for everyone on our planet is this, "May God Bless You, and All Who Stride With You."

This will do as a closing for now, but it seems slightly long and may well have to be edited down.

Continuing with planning of my talk, how do I want to open my talk? What kind of opening should I select? Drawing from chapter 10 "Opening Your Speech" the purpose of the opening is to capture the audience's attention and interest, and to have them thinking "Tell me more," or "This is going to be good." Of the many types of openings, the circular opening, and the story opening are my favorites. However, this speech is too short to open with a story and also cover my background, interests, and ambitions systematically. Consequently, I will settle for a quotation opening, and use the same quotation to transition into the body.

Recall these heuristics; the audience will decide in the first seven seconds whether or not they like you; the audience will decide in the first thirty seconds if they want to tune in or tune out. These decisions will be made subconsciously. This is the window of opportunity. Don't blow it by not planning and rehearsing diligently.

A reminder: Effective openings should achieve some of the following. They should introduce the topic, capture attention, and establish rapport. This can be achieved by asking rhetorical questions, making shocking statements, using stories, or opening with quotations, etc.

One of my favorite quotations is athlete Steve Prefontaine's, *"To give anything less than your best is to sacrifice the gift."* I will attempt an opening with this—also to set a standard and expectancy of excellence.

Tentative opening.

(Opening quotation) *To give anything less than your best, is to sacrifice the gift. This is a fairly famous quote. Over the years I, however, have come to view this more as a code of conduct; a strictly optional one.*

(Greeting, road map, and transition to first point—background) *Mr./Ms. Toastmaster, ladies and gentlemen; today I, Rashid N. Kapadia,* (I would remove my name if the Toastmaster or the person who introduced me has already told the audience my name) *have been tasked with introducing myself by sharing my background, my interests, and my ambitions with all of you. Over the next five minutes I will stay true to this code of conduct, and give it my best shot.*

My background could safely be summarized by these words.

I am a fortunate man.

At this point I would make the title of my talk, "A Fortunate Man." Also I would commit to memorizing the opening—it is easy enough.

The structure I will follow for this speech is: strong opening, transition (greeting and road map), point 1 (background), transition, point 2 (interests), transition, point 3 (ambitions), transition to close, strong close.

Tentatively my speech looks like this.

A Fortunate Man

Strong Opening

(Opening quotation) *To give anything less than your best, is to sacrifice the gift. This is a fairly famous quote. Over the years I, however, have come to view this more as a code of conduct; a strictly optional one.*

(Greeting, road map, and transition to first point— background) *Mr./Ms. Toastmaster, ladies and gentlemen; today I have been tasked with introducing myself by sharing my background, my interests, and my ambitions with all of you. Over the next five minutes I will stay true to this code of conduct, and give it my best shot.*

My background could safely be summarized by these words. I am a fortunate man.

Point 1

Talk about my background

Transition to point 2

That's my background. Here are my interests.

Point 2

Talk about my interests

Transition to point 3

My ambitions; past, present and future, may be subtitled, "Three Resets."

Point 3

Talk about my ambitions.

Transition into close.

A maritime tradition, dating back thousands of years, calls for a ceremonial blessing when a newly-built ship is launched from land to sea for the first time, "May God Bless Her and All Who Sail in Her."

Strong close.

Now, as I begin yet another new voyage, may I shamelessly ask you for a gift. A gift that will cost you neither time nor treasure. I ask for your good wishes. More than anything else, I seek your good wishes. And if these should be granted easily, and generously, then may I ask for more, may I ask for your blessings.

I know in a way that is non-negotiable, that all of us, whether we are speakers on a stage, or slum dwellers in squalor, or even if we are sovereigns of state, one way or another, we are all in the same boat; together.

And one way or another, now and always, my wish for each and every one of you, indeed for everyone on our planet is this, "May God Bless You, and All Who Stride With You."

Looking at this draft, it is about 300 words, without the content for the three main points. I have to constrain the speech to no more than 750 words, preferably 500-600 words, so I already have my first challenge—too much content, too many words.

If you recall, this is the first issue. This is the most common beginner's mistake. Trying to put in too much information. It's happening right here, and I've hardly started.

You may recall that I recommended an HBR article in

chapter 5: "Basic Parts of a Speech" (Harvard Business Review: How to Give a Killer Presentation: Lessons from TED by Chris Anderson: June 2013 REPRINT R1306K)

From the article: *The biggest problem I see in first drafts of presentations is that they try to cover too much ground. You can't summarize an entire career in a single talk. If you try to cram in everything you know, you won't have time to include key details ... So limit the scope of your talk to that which can be explained, and brought to life with examples, in the available time. Much of the early feedback we give aims to correct the impulse to sweep too broadly ... Don't tell us about your entire field of study—tell us about your unique contribution.*

Here's your chance not to make the first and most common mistake.

Anyway, let me proceed to Point 1: My background. Here I revisit my written story and reduce it big-time, without losing its essence. Let me give it a try.

I was born in India and was fortunate to be raised in a family surrounded by love and contentment. I am fortunate that my parents set stellar standards and set sterling examples. I am fortunate to have two wonderful sisters, and even more fortunate to have an identical twin brother. My super-special relationship with my twin once more proves my premise: indeed, I am "A Fortunate Man."

I went to an excellent boarding school; the seeds of self-reliance were sown there. I completed a marine engineering apprenticeship program. I sailed as a marine engineer for more than a decade.

Anahita and I were married in 1985; together we have shared many unique voyages. We are "A Blessed Couple." That we are. We have a son, Rehan: He is the single greatest blessing and joy in our life. Our treasure with no parallel.

In 1995, the three of us moved from India to the United

States.

This is another 150 words.

Point 2: My interests

Reading, learning, leading, building, pushing boundaries of both knowledge and performance ... and public speaking.

I am interested in always having excellent human relationships with all.

I am interested in pushing myself and others around me toward twin North Stars called ENTERPRISE & EXCELLENCE.

As an immigrant US citizen I am deeply interested in doing my bit toward forming a more perfect union.

This is another 60 words.

A comment: I deliberately did not mention my interest in evangelizing PS&ST to PM&Es because I do not want any element of "selling my book" to be part of this speech. There will be an appropriate time and opportunity for that later. This is a choice I have made, and I will stay with it.

Point 3: My ambitions

In 1985, I took an unusual chance. I put all my life savings into a marine engineering certification course in the United Kingdom. Had I failed ... well I don't even want to think of the consequences. Fortunately, I prevailed. I now think of this as a Reset moment: a moment of pointing my compass in a different direction.

A decade later, 1995, I reset my compass once again. I'll call it Reset 2. With family in tow, with my entire life savings on the line, I moved to the US as a graduate student and took on an ambitious study program. I now look back at this one year of intense study as a career sabbatical. The future was uncertain; there were no guarantees. Fortunately, I prevailed.

Now almost two decades later, I pressed the Reset button again. I'll call it Reset 3. In April 2014, I left my job to begin another nine-month career sabbatical, mindful of significant financial challenges.

I intend to focus on developing my writing and speaking skills.

At the end of this sabbatical I must have a prototype: some combination of products or services that are both unique and valuable. And I must have completed writing and publishing a book.

All going well, at the end of this sabbatical, I will begin a new voyage; one of entrepreneurship.

This point is about 230 words.

So right now I am looking at a total of about 750 words (300 open, transitions, and close; 150 point 1; 60 point 2; and 230 point 3). Not too bad. But I still want to reduce it to around 600 words if possible. This means at my preferred speaking rate of 100 words per minute, I will finish in six minutes.

This part, removing the excess from the speech, is both the most agonizing and the most fun part of the editing work. The idea is to remove anything that does not directly tie into the core message.

Here we go.

Edit 1

(Opening quotation) *To give anything less than your best, is to sacrifice the gift. This is a fairly famous quote. Over the years I, however, have come to view this more as a code of conduct; a strictly optional one.*

 Changed to

To give anything less than your best, is to sacrifice the gift. A famous quote; and a personal motto.

Edit 2

(Greeting, road map, and transition to first point— background) *Mr./Ms. Toastmaster, ladies and gentlemen; today I have been tasked with introducing myself by sharing my background, my interests, and my ambitions with all of you. Over the next five minutes I will stay true to this code of conduct, and give it my best shot.*

My background could safely be summarized by these words. I am a fortunate man.

Changed to

Mr./Ms. Toastmaster, ladies and gentlemen; I have been tasked with introducing myself by sharing my background, my interests, and my ambitions. I refuse to give anything less than my best to this task.

My background in few words: I am a fortunate man.

Edit 3

(Point 1)

I was born in India and was fortunate to be raised in a family surrounded by love and contentment. I am fortunate that my parents set stellar standards and set sterling examples. I am fortunate to have two wonderful sisters, and even more fortunate to have an identical twin brother. My super-special relationship with my twin once more proves my premise: indeed, I am "A Fortunate Man."

I went to an excellent boarding school; here the seeds of self-reliance were sown. I completed a marine engineering apprenticeship program. I sailed as a marine engineer for more than a decade.

Anahita and I were married in 1985; together we have shared many unique voyages. We are "A Blessed Couple." That we are. We have a son Rehan: he is the single greatest blessing and joy in our life. Our treasure with no parallel.

In 1995, the three of us moved from India to the United States.

Changed to

Born in India … fortunate to be raised in a family surrounded by love and contentment. Fortunate that my parents set stellar standards and set sterling examples. Fortunate to have two wonderful sisters, and an identical twin brother. My relationship with my twin is super-special.

I went to an excellent boarding school. I completed a marine engineering apprenticeship program. I sailed as a marine engineer for more than a decade.

Anahita and I were married in 1985; together we have shared many unique voyages. We are "A Blessed Couple." We have a son Rehan: he is the single greatest blessing and joy in our life. Our treasure with no parallel.

In 1995, the three of us moved from India to the United States.

No edit here

Transition to point 2

That's my background. Here are my interests.

No edit here

(Point 2) *Reading, learning, leading, building, pushing boundaries of both knowledge and performance ... and public speaking.*

I am interested in always having excellent human relationships with all.

I am interested in pushing myself and others around me toward twin North Stars called ENTERPRISE & EXCELLENCE.

As an immigrant US citizen, I am deeply interested in doing my bit toward forming a more perfect union.

No edit here

Transition to point 3

My ambitions; past, present and future, may be subtitled, "Three Resets."

Edit 4

(Point 3) *In 1985, I took an unusual chance. I put all my life savings into a marine engineering certification course in the United Kingdom. Had I failed ... well I don't even want to think of the consequences. Fortunately, I prevailed. I now think of* this as a Reset moment: a moment of pointing my compass in a different direction.

A decade later, 1995, I reset my compass once again. I'll call it Reset 2. With family in tow, with my entire life savings on the line, I moved to the US as a graduate student and took on an ambitious study program. I now look back at this one year of intense study as a career sabbatical. The future was uncertain; there were no guarantees. Fortunately, I prevailed.

Now almost two decades later, I pressed the Reset button again. I'll call it Reset 3. In April 2014, I left my job to begin another nine-month career sabbatical, mindful of significant financial hardships.

I intend to focus on developing my writing and speaking skills.

At the end of this sabbatical I must have a prototype: some combination of products or services that are both unique and valuable. And I must have completed writing and publishing a book.

All going well, at the end of this sabbatical, I will begin a new voyage; one of entrepreneurship.

Changed to

In 1985, I took an unusual chance. I put all my life savings into a marine engineering certification course in the United Kingdom. Had I failed … well I don't even want to think of the consequences. Fortunately, I prevailed. I now think of this as a Reset moment.

A decade later, 1995, I reset once again: Reset 2. With family in tow, with my entire life savings on the line, I moved to the US as a graduate student and took on an ambitious study program. I now look back at this one year of intense study as a career sabbatical. The future was uncertain; there were no guarantees. Fortunately, I prevailed.

Now almost two decades later, I pressed the Reset button

again. I'll call it Reset 3. In April 2014, I left my job to begin another nine-month career sabbatical, mindful of significant financial hardships.

I intend to focus on developing my writing and speaking skills, and complete writing and publishing a book.

All going well, at the end of this sabbatical, I will begin a new voyage; one of entrepreneurship.

Edit 5

Transition into close

A maritime tradition, dating back thousands of years, calls for a ceremonial blessing when a newly-built ship is launched from land to sea for the first time, "May God Bless Her and All Who Sail in Her."

Changed to

An ancient maritime tradition calls for a ceremonial blessing when a newly-built ship is first launched. "May God Bless Her and All Who Sail in Her."

I will try to keep the conclusion intact. Hopefully no editing required. Let us see.

No Edit

Strong close

Now, as I begin yet another new voyage, may I shamelessly ask you for a gift. A gift that will cost you neither time nor treasure. I ask for your good wishes. More than anything else, I seek your good wishes. And if these should be granted easily, and generously, then may I ask for more, may I ask for your blessings.

I know in a way that is non-negotiable, that all of us, whether we are speakers on a stage, or slum dwellers in squalor, or even if we are sovereigns of state, one way or another, we are all in the same boat; together.

And one way or another, now and always, my wish for each and every one of you, indeed for everyone on our planet is this,

"May God Bless You, and All Who Stride With You."
Now let's see where we stand.

A Fortunate Man

Strong Opening
To give anything less than your best, is to sacrifice the gift. A famous quote; and a personal motto.

Greeting, road map, and transition to first point—background
Mr./Ms. Toastmaster, ladies and gentlemen; I have been tasked with introducing myself by sharing my background, my interests, and my ambitions. I refuse to give anything less than my best to this task.

My background in few words: I am a fortunate man.

Point 1
Born in India ... fortunate to be raised in a family surrounded by love and contentment. Fortunate that my parents set stellar standards and set sterling examples. Fortunate to have two wonderful sisters, and an identical twin brother. My relationship with my twin is super-special.

I went to an excellent boarding school. I completed a marine engineering apprenticeship program. I sailed as a marine engineer for more than a decade.

Anahita and I were married in 1985; together we have shared many unique voyages. We are "A Blessed Couple." We have a son Rehan: he is the single greatest blessing and joy in our life. Our treasure with no parallel.

In 1995, the three of us moved from India to the United States.

Transition to point 2
That's my background. Here are my interests.

Point 2

Reading, learning, leading, building, pushing boundaries of both knowledge and performance ... and public speaking.

I am interested in always having excellent human relationships with all.

I am interested in pushing myself and others around me toward twin North Stars called ENTERPRISE & EXCELLENCE.

As an immigrant US citizen I am deeply interested in doing my bit toward forming a more perfect union.

Transition to point 3

My ambitions; past, present and future, may be subtitled, "Three Resets."

Point 3

In 1985, I took an unusual chance. I put all my life savings into a marine engineering certification course in the United Kingdom. Had I failed ... well I don't even want to think of the consequences. Fortunately, I prevailed. I now think of this as a Reset moment.

A decade later, 1995, I reset once again: Reset 2. With family in tow, with my entire life savings on the line, I moved to the US as a graduate student and took on an ambitious study program. I now look back at this one year of intense study as a career sabbatical. The future was uncertain; there were no guarantees. Fortunately, I prevailed.

Now almost two decades later, I pressed the Reset button again. I'll call it Reset 3. In April 2014, I left my job to begin another nine-month career sabbatical, mindful of significant financial hardships.

I intend to focus on developing my writing and speaking skill, and complete writing and publishing a book.

All going well, at the end of this sabbatical, I will begin a new voyage; one of entrepreneurship.

Transition into close

An ancient maritime tradition calls for a ceremonial blessing when a newly built ship is first launched. "May God Bless Her and All Who Sail in Her."

Strong close

Now, as I begin yet another new voyage, may I shamelessly ask you for a gift. A gift that will cost you neither time nor treasure. I ask for your good wishes. More than anything else, I seek your good wishes. And if these should be granted easily, and generously, then may I ask for more, may I ask for your blessings.

I know in a way that is non-negotiable, that all of us, whether we are speakers on a stage, or slum dwellers in squalor, or even if we are sovereigns of state, one way or another, we are all in the same boat; together.

And one way or another, now and always, my wish for each and every one of you, indeed for everyone on our planet is this, "May God Bless You, and All Who Stride With You."

We are now at about 620 words. I can accept this.

I am willing to remove this line if I sense time constraints.

I am interested in pushing myself and others around me toward twin North Stars called ENTERPRISE & EXCELLENCE.

If I absolutely have to, I can remove this paragraph from the conclusion—though I would hate to.

I know in a way that is non-negotiable, that all of us, whether we are speakers on a stage, or slum dwellers in squalor, or even if we are sovereigns of state, one way or another, we are all in the same boat; together.

This would bring the total to 555-575 words. So I am fine. If I sense I am seriously running out of time, I can remove this paragraph. If not, I will definitely keep it in.

Hope you have done this exercise in parallel with me. If not, plan to return and do it.

Your next step would be to give the speech, raw as it is,

and actively solicit feedback.

I printed out this exact speech and without any further preparation or memorization, I gave it in one of my Toastmasters clubs. I was willing to read a bit if necessary, as this was a deliberate work in progress, not a finished product.

The feedback I got was most helpful. Fortunately I had an excellent, experienced, and insightful evaluator who did not shirk from his responsibility to provide very real feedback. Three main points:

1. My delivery had too much "sameness." Compared with some of my earlier speeches my club members had heard, this one lacked vocal variety and naturalness: It sounded more forced and overformal—not like an effortless or a one-to-one conversation.

2. The transitions did not come off well. Sounded rigid and lacked smoothness—especially from point 1 to point 2, i.e. background to interests.

3. Reading from my notes (I read very little) should be avoided. My club members have seen me speak without notes regularly—and commented that reading, however little, was noticeable and took away something. Note that I was using the Churchill/Roosevelt/Reagan method described in chapter 4. I was not speaking when looking down to read. Still, it took away something.

Very good feedback. Thank You!

I know there is much more room for improvement. There always will be. That is how it should be. I will have to keep refining. This is not close to where it can be. Remember the asymptote approach. For now it is "good enough" and that is good enough. Ted Sorensen, the legendary speechwriter, counselor, and alter ego to President John F. Kennedy, produced amazing results by following a simple formula. He taught that a great speech should strive to include four basic elements. Clarity. Brevity. Levity. Charity. My icebreaker falls clearly short on levity. More work to be done!

There is yet another step to be followed, but I will only briefly touch upon it here. Record yourself speaking (not reading) and then transcribe the speech. This means it should be written down exactly as it was spoken; word for word. This becomes your newest script. Edit the parts that you do not like, but then speak the newly edited parts aloud to ensure that the editing is representative of the way you speak, not the way you write. If you follow all these steps, you will have a solid foundation from which you can consistently draw material for future speeches. Congratulations and well done.

This was another long chapter, but necessarily so. Lots of iterations are part of the process. In this chapter you have seen only two iterations. In the real world there should be many more.

I occasionally work with others, helping them to improve their speeches. It is not uncommon to go to version 10 or more. Only minor changes no doubt, but continuous improvement based on practice, feedback, and coaching results in multiple changes. This is the desirable way forward.

Here are some parts directly from the book *Emote: Using Emotions to Make Your Message Memorable* by Vikas Jhingran, that I highlighted.

A speech when first conceived is rarely as beautiful as it ends up. Sometimes the final emotion, or the key idea is the only thing that remains from the original version.

The process of refining from the first draft to the final version of the speech is really where great speakers distinguish themselves.

The whole process of refining a speech is to get an alignment between the emotional journey of the audience and the emotional journey that was planned by the speaker.

If these messages and this approach are beginning to resonate more with you now, once again I recommend you put it in your project plan to procure books like *Emote*. Syntopical reading is an excellent way toward mastery.

Sometimes we may be asked some personal questions after a talk, or during an interview. We should prepare for this too— beyond the background, interests, ambitions model of the icebreaker. Personal questions are best answered by the "tell a (personal) story: make a point" approach. You can answer with: "For example, this happened to me (tell the story) and then add and that is how I learned (describe in one sentence, the lesson learned) this."

Now I want to briefly return to the subjects of politics, religion, and sex. I know I said I would discuss them no further. But I want to make a point. I included them in chapter 1 for a very specific reason. That I would be prepared with an answer, if questions relating to them were ever thrown my way—and I felt the best response would be to answer them. Using a "hope for the best, prepare for the worst approach," it is a good idea for every speaker who expects to be asked questions to be prepared for inappropriate, even hostile, questions without stumbling.

Following up with the "be an idealist without illusions" approach, it is realistic to presume that you will inevitably be at the receiving end of hostile questions, or questions that are designed to ensnare, entrap, and make you look incompetent or untrustworthy. Just look at some of the more provocative shows on TV. It is a part of our existence that some audiences gravitate toward this. Hostile and "trip you up" questions may, by design, be part of a tough interview too. I acknowledge that in a perfect world they should not be, but we are not in a perfect world. Best to be prepared for these, too. Don't get flustered, outraged, or similar. Respond with practiced and politically correct answers that represent your fundamental truth. Then transition by taking control of the situation and steer the questioner firmly away, with soft eye contact, and a kind closing comment "and that's my last word on politics, religion, or sex. Period."

In today's world the reality is that increasingly we are all required to join, or lead new teams, more frequently than in the past. With virtual teams being a new normal, with teams being put together for only the duration of projects, the ability to rapidly build trust is a new distinguishing competency. Being prepared with an excellent and sincere icebreaker speech, and with personal stories, is a successful way to initiate the process of rapidly building trust.

Here is my *eleventh wish* for you: May your icebreaker speech be one, which your entire family is proud of, and one, which has the potential to rapidly build trust. Good luck!

Chapter 15

Memorizing, Listening, and Connecting

This chapter is about memorizing your speeches, listening to your audiences, and connecting with your audiences. It will be brief and will mostly consist of evangelizing these three topics, introducing the basics, and pointing to external resources for more inspiration and information.

I believe that, for some readers, chapter 6, "The Fittest Speaker, The Expert Speaker" could be the most important chapter in this book. I will now argue that this chapter could be the second most important one.

Much as I have evangelized PS&ST throughout this book, I will acknowledge that if you become an expert at memorizing, listening, and connecting, then you will be better served in life and profession than if you become an expert in PS&ST.

It is really, really hard to become an expert memorizer, listener, and connector.

If you commit to acquiring expertise in memorizing, listening, and connecting, then I suggest you will require more concentration of will, even more energy of soul than any other part that your PS&ST voyage will require of you. Do you recall this line from chapter 4? *We choose to do these things ... not because they are easy ... but because they are hard.* It is from JFK's "We Choose To Go To The Moon" speech. Well, this would be the most appropriate time to draw all the inspiration you can from it.

And like everything that is hard and must be pursued with devotion, concentration of will, and energy of soul, the reward is correspondingly great.

Dear reader, I hope you commit to taking the voyage toward acquiring expertise in memorizing, listening, and connecting. You have been warned. It is much harder than anything else associated with PS&ST.

Memorizing, listening, and connecting are not absolutely necessary toward becoming an expert public speaker and storyteller. I suspect that there are many world class public speakers and storytellers who are not experts in memorization, listening, or connecting; and they are simultaneously really good speakers and storytellers! But being able to deeply listen to your audience and deeply connect with your audience is an expertise that is supremely worthy of your pursuit. In my opinion this ought to be one of the highest aspirations of PS&ST. This is where the sport, the art, and the science of PS&ST transform into the heaven of service. Here's a Rabindranath Tagore quote I learned in my school days:

I slept and dreamt that life was joy.
I awoke and saw that life was service.
I acted, and behold, service was joy.

Memorizing

"If we want to live memorable lives ...
we have to remember to remember."
— Joshua Foer, TED Talk

I remember my jaw dropping when I started reading Joshua Foer's book, *Moonwalking with Einstein: The Art and Science of Remembering Everything.* It is one of the best books I have recently read. I suggest it should be compulsory reading for everyone who wishes to grow in life. If you have children, nieces, or nephews, gift each of them a copy. Worst outcome is that they will not read it. If they do, the benefits have the potential to be life-altering. Here is the key reason: "Our lives are the sum of our memories."

Joshua Foer is a science journalist who made an extraordinary one-year voyage. As part of his science journalism job, he decided to cover a USA memory championship event.

Preparing for the event, he read a newspaper interview with Ben Pridmore.

In the book, *Moonwalking with Einstein,* he writes: *Ben Pridmore could memorize the order of a shuffled deck of playing cards in thirty-two seconds. In five minutes he could permanently commit to memory what happened on ninety-six different historical dates.* **The man knew fifty thousand digits of pi.**

In the newspaper interview Ben Pridmore insists: *"It's all about technique and understanding how memory works. Anyone can do it really."*

Anyone can remember fifty thousand digits of pi? Anyone can do it?! Really??!!

Joshua Foer attended the 2005 USA Memory Championship at Con Edison headquarters near Union Square in Manhattan. After the event he met some of the contestants and champions, and started talking to them. In his own words: *What I discovered as I talked to the competitors was something far more serious, a story that made me reconsider the limits of my own mind and the **very essence of my education**.*

He asked one of the memory experts, a young grandmaster from England, Ed Cooke: *"When did you first realize you were a savant?"*

"Oh, I'm not a savant." Ed replied, chuckling.

Joshua Foer persisted, "Photographic memory?"

Ed chuckled again, "Photographic memory doesn't exist. It is a detestable myth. In fact my memory is quite average. All of us here have average memories."

Joshua Foer had just watched Ed Cooke recite 252 random numbers as effortlessly as if they had been his own telephone number. How does one reconcile this fact with what Ed Cooke was claiming?

Ed continued, "What you have to understand is that even

average memories are remarkably powerful if used properly."

Joshua Foer goes on to write: *Ed and all the other mental athletes I met kept insisting, as Ben Pridmore has in his interview, that anyone could do what they do. It was simply a matter of* **"learning to think in more memorable ways"** *using the* **"extraordinarily simple"** *2500-year–old mnemonic technique known as the* **"memory palace"** *that Simonides of Ceos had supposedly invented in the rubble of a great banquet hall collapse in Greece in 5th century BC.*

Ed Cooke explained to Joshua Foer that the competitors saw themselves as participants in an amateur research program whose aim was to rescue a long-lost tradition of memory training that had disappeared for centuries. Once upon a time, Ed insisted, remembering was everything.

Ed and Joshua's conversation led to Joshua contemplating becoming a memory athlete himself. Ed offered to coach him.

Joshua Foer accepted the offer and the challenge. He trained with diligence and determination. He worked with the expert on expertise Anders Ericsson. Remember him from chapter 6? Joshua Foer researched memory deeply. He committed to being an expert student. And he **won the 2006 USA Memory Championship**! This is a truly amazing story.

Please plan on watching this TED Talk sooner, rather than later.

Joshua Foer: "Feats of memory that anyone can do"
http://www.ted.com/talks/joshua_foer_feats_of_memory_anyone_can_do#t-7141

The talk ends with this sage advice. *I learned firsthand that there are incredible memory capacities latent in all of us. But if you want to live a memorable life, you have to be the kind of person who remembers to remember.*

In my opinion, there are two key insights to grasp on the road to a better-trained memory.

- We remember (1) routes and (2) powerful visual images best. To remember anything, put the components on a route. This is called a "memory palace." Next associate the individual components with outrageous images. We saw Joshua Foer do just this in his TED Talk.
- Convert Baker (a name) to baker (an image). This is a creative and fun process, not a memorization and tedious process.

Here's a personal story. Shortly after I read this book, I was at a PMI-Houston Conference, and attended a memory-training breakout session. The instructor challenged the attendees to remember a random list of 15 items. He asked for a volunteer to recall the list aloud. I volunteered to try. To my utter shock (and I am being neither modest nor gracious) I remembered every item correctly, in correct order. The whole room started clapping—implying that I was very smart. I certainly am not very smart. I certainly do not have a special or trained memory. I was simultaneously bewildered and having a revelation! This was an eye-opener for me. I do not remember remembering a 15-item list from memory for decades, if ever. What I did was place each item systematically in a location of my childhood home, and create a strong visual with each item. The instructor asked how I remembered the list and I mentioned I read the book *Moonwalking with Einstein* recently and decided to try out the memory palace technique. He was familiar with the book and concurred that all memory training is based on similar approaches.

This boosted my confidence significantly. I decided to try and use this approach for memorizing my speeches. I report to you that it works very well. Go for it. You can do it!

I serendipitously discovered a huge bonus benefit associated with a memorized speech. When I have a speech memorized,

I am able to say each sentence looking straight into the eyes (and heart) of an audience member. This ability of saying one sentence to one audience member, the next sentence to another, the third to yet another audience member, takes the speech to a completely different level of communication. It is a marvelous feeling. And it gives you the ability to listen to your audience and to draw energy from them.

Once you start speaking this way, you may never want to go back to any other way.

Here are some common questions.

1. Should we memorize a speech?
2. Is it worth the effort?
3. Is it necessary/essential to memorize a speech?
4. Does it really matter to the audience if we have the speech memorized?

I do not claim to have either correct or definitive answers. I recommend that you experiment and decide for yourself. My recommendation: Experiment boldly.

Let me make a few comments:

1. It is OK to read from notes. It is not OK to "look-down-and-read-and-speak" simultaneously. If you have to read, then pledge to yourself that you will always use the Churchill/Roosevelt/Reagan method described in chapter 4. This is the minimum you owe the audience. It's not about you! And make the same promise if you are using slides with lots of text. If you simply have to look at the slides as a mnemonic, then at the very least do not speak when looking at the slides. Take a mental snapshot of some text, turn and face your audience, pause, speak (conversationalize) to one person, and then repeat the cycle. This is deeply uncomfortable for you the speaker, but it is much, much better for the audience. So accept the discomfort by committing to serve your audience. It's not that tough. All it takes is practice. You can do it!

2. If you chose not to memorize your speech, then you will compromise your ability to draw energy from your audience, to really listen to your audience, or to more fully connect with your audience.

3. If you chose not to memorize your entire speech, but you are willing to memorize parts of it, then commit to this. Memorize the very first sentence and the very last sentence. If you can take on more, memorize the first two sentences and the last two sentences. And it you feel that you can take on still more, then memorize the entire opening, the entire closing, and the transitions. And if you can take on still more, then memorize the quotations and any planned "magic moments." These are the moments when you connect deeply with your audience, or are your core messages, or punch lines, or profound insights, or important lessons.

In my experience, the greatest benefit of memorizing a speech is that it frees you up to pay evermore attention to your audience. You now have mental resources available to listen to them, to sense their response, to capture their attention, and to draw in their energy. All too often, when we are not optimally prepared with our speeches, we do not remember what we said, and we certainly have no idea of what the audience took away. All our attention was directed inward. This is not the optimal way to serve our audiences.

Now let us transition to listening.

Oh, one last thing, before I forget. I strongly recommend that you procure and study the book *Moonwalking with Einstein*. Commit to an analytical reading of this book. Get the elementary reading and inspectional reading out of the way and then do a very thorough reading of this book. Good luck!

Listening

"Wisdom is the reward you get for a lifetime
of listening when you'd have preferred to talk."
— Doug Larson

Directing attention to the importance of listening was one of the serendipitous benefits I got from my PS&ST voyage. I sense this is another area in which a lot of new knowledge is emerging.

I remember being intrigued and fascinated when watching Julian Treasure's TED Talks. It was the same feeling I had when reading Sandra Zimmer's *It's Your Time To Shine*, or Vikas Jhingran's *Emote* for the first time. Here's a trailblazer. Here is new knowledge (at least for me) that is outside the usual PS&ST material I come across. I think it is really important for public speakers and storytellers to know all this.

At a convenient opportunity, when you can block out about 45 minutes, I ask that you listen to all these Julian Treasure @ TED Talks with an open mind, like a sponge, absorbing all you can. Please put this into your project plan.

"Five ways to listen better"
http://www.ted.com/talks/julian_treasure_5_ways_to_listen_better
"How to speak so that people want to listen"
http://www.ted.com/talks/julian_treasure_how_to_speak_so_that_people_want_to_listen
"Sound health in eight steps"
http://www.ted.com/talks/julian_treasure_shh_sound_health_in_8_steps
"The four ways sound affects us"
http://www.ted.com/talks/julian_treasure_the_4_ways_

sound_affects_us
"Why architects need to use their ears"
http://www.ted.com/talks/julian_treasure_why_
architects_need_to_use_their_ears

As communicators, we can perhaps compare PS&ST to throwing a ball. Our responsibility is to throw the ball. It is the audience member's responsibility to catch the ball. How we throw the ball makes a huge difference. Knowing the catcher's catching ability increases the odds that the ball will be caught. Do you agree?

These five talks have made me more aware of the catcher's needs, abilities, and habits. I hope they do the same for you.

After listening to all of Julian Treasure's talks, it became clear to me that there is also a third element: The environment in which the ball is being passed.

When considering the listening aspect of your speech or presentation, do not be unmindful that your best efforts and intentions can be hopelessly compromised by you not being sound-environment savvy.

Listening skills are getting more and more attention as relationship and performance enhancers. I do not intend to go over them here. There are plenty of good books and training material available for this. I recommend you consider getting one or more of these.

I'll include a recommendation. *Search Inside Yourself: The Unexpected Path to Achieving Success, Happiness (and World Peace)* by Chade-Meng Tan. Specifically, I will recommend you do the listening EXERCISES in chapters 3 & 7. I particularly like this book as it contains a lot of insights, even deep wisdom, while maintaining a playful, practical, and humorous overtone. And I particularly like the fact that the author is an engineer.

You are probably familiar with these terms; passive listening, active listening, mindful listening, cognitive listening, empathetic listening, etc. I now believe there is one more type of listening that is even harder than any of these. The ability of a speaker to listen to an audience.

Most of us, most of the time, cannot remember what we said in our speeches, especially our earlier speeches. With practice and commitment (and yes, stage time, stage time, stage time: thank you, Darren LaCroix) we get more comfortable and have a fairly good recall of what we said, but we do not really know how the audience received it. This is the next level. If you know how each member of the audience received and absorbed your speech, then you have mastered what I think may be the most difficult of all listening skills. This is more practical and achievable with smaller audiences.

An advantage of attempting to master this type of listening (i.e. listening to your audience deeply even as you are speaking) is that it will probably catalyze the learning of all your other listening skills as well.

This is not as esoteric as it sounds. This too requires practice and commitment.

I got exposed to this concept (listening deeply to your audience) through the work of Sandra Zimmer and Lee Glickstein. Through their books I came to accept that this is a skill that can be attained practically. Lee Glickstein's book is called *Be Heard Now! Tap into Your Inner Speaker and Communicate with Ease.* It is an unusual and splendid book. It has my recommendation for you to procure.

I have included a part of this book as my pre-speech-preparation notes. I refer to them very frequently and it helps me to remember.

- *It's all about Relational Presence.*
- *We have to forget about being good, and remember to be*

ourselves.
- *They do not care what you know until they know that you care.*
- **The key to connecting with any audience is not knowing how to give to them—but knowing how to receive support from them.**
- *Message is important—but the depth of our commitment to that message, and our relationship with our audience is even more important.*
- **Develop capacity to listen while speaking, to both my audience and myself. Key element of success is listening with no agenda. Listen attentively with soft and available eyes.**
- **It is our receptivity that draws people to us.**
- **Energy going out and energy coming in are both really the same ... it is connection.**

This too is from *Be Heard Now*:

3 x Basic Steps to Connecting With Any Audience.
1. *Stand with your feet planted into the center of the earth— and listen to your audience before you begin speaking.*
2. *Speak clearly, from the heart, in short sentences. Say every sentence into the eyes and heart of a human being in the audience.*
3. *Spend 5–10 seconds of quality time with each listener before moving on to another.*

It is my hope that I have adequately evangelized the option of listening deeply to your audience. I hope at some point on your PS&ST voyage you will get there. This part of the voyage will require concentration of will and energy of soul. Good luck! You can do it!

Connecting

I'll keep this section very brief. Connection is the most ineffable, most visceral, and most immeasurable of all the experiences I have had on my PS&ST voyage.

I believe there is a universal hunger for connection, which has roots in some form of ancient neural programming. I am speculating that it is an evolutionary bequeath that we are grasping at, and only beginning to decode. I will not be too surprised if some time in the future "survival of the fittest" will be upgraded to "survival of the best-connected."

I am guessing that every family, every community, every group of people—be it a state, a country or a continent—feels (and yearns for) some sort of connection.

Coming unapologetically from a rational and engineering background, I remain optimistic that we will increasingly understand the origins and mechanisms of connection, will be able to increasingly harness its bounty, and we will be more able to measure it.

Here are two statements I have not come across before and think to be accurate and relevant.

1. PS&ST are connection enablers.
2. PS&ST are "flow" enablers.
   (More in the next chapter.)

For me, these are two ultimate goals associated with my PS&ST voyage. I will strive to be an expert PS&ST, knowing that as a result I will be an expert and effortless connector. I will strive for PS&ST expertise with the goal of being able to get into the flow state when communicating.

Neural resonance (the term I was introduced to by Daniel Goleman's work, and discussed in chapter 8, "Ending Your Speech") is the best way for me to understand connection.

The ultimate objective of every speech, every presentation, every story, and indeed every communication, should be neural resonance. I have never heard of this as being the ultimate objective of PS&ST, but I believe it should be. It certainly is mine.

A day may come when neural patterns of speaker and audience can effectively be monitored and measured. If that happens, (PM&Es will be at the forefront of that effort) I am speculating that the more similar the neural patterns, the greater the neural resonance, the more successful the speech will have been judged to be. Put differently, I suspect that correlation between neural resonance and successful PS&ST is high.

So, dear PM&E, please consider making neural resonance the ultimate objective of your PS&ST voyage. Perhaps, the greatest benefit you get from your PS&ST voyage is an upgraded ability to connect instantly and effortlessly with your audiences, indeed with all who are a part of your lives— on and off stage.

Here is my *twelfth wish* for you. May your PS&ST voyage culminate in you becoming an expert memorizer, an expert listener, an expert connector and an expert at generating neural resonance.

Chapter 16

Finding Flow Through Public Speaking and Storytelling

*"Don't ask what the world needs. Ask what
makes you come alive. Because what the world
needs most is more people who have come alive."*
— Howard Thurman

PS&ST make me come alive. Setting clear goals and moving toward them make me come alive. The marvels of engineering make me come alive. Some challenges associated with difficult projects make me come alive. Wonderful relationships make me come alive. Marvelous conversations make me come alive. Being part of a high-energy, positive group that is working toward self-improvement makes me come alive. The list goes on. Watching JFK's "We Choose to Go to the Moon" speech makes me come alive. Watching the movie "On Human Destiny" at Space Center Houston makes me come alive. I understand that what all these may have in common, for me, is that they get me into some kind of low-grade-flow-state, and it is this combination state-of-body-and-state-of-mind that makes me feel alive.

Not surprisingly, I had heard of the flow state off and on over the years, especially associated with athletes, musicians, and performers. After listening to Martin Seligman's TED Talk "The new era of positive psychology," I began to investigate it more seriously.

Seligman suggests that there are three different sources of happiness, which are the pleasant life (positive emotions, positive affectation), the good life (engagement, seeking mastery, working from your highest strengths), and the meaningful life (contributing to a purpose that is greater than you). He goes on to describe those who experience the good life as being enormously capable of flow. He refers to Mike Csikszentmihalyi's TED Talk. I listened to it. Once again I knew that I was in the presence of a trailblazer. For me this was new knowledge. This led me to Csikszentmihalyi's book, *Flow: The Psychology of Optimal Experience.*

If you are not familiar with *Flow*, plan on watching Csikszentmihalyi's TED Talk, "Flow, the secret to happiness." Syntopically reading the transcript along with this chapter, now or later, is a good idea. http://www.ted.com/talks/ mihaly_csikszentmihalyi_on_flow

This was my introduction to Flow, and it stayed dormant in my memory until I heard Fareed Zakaria (a CNN television talk show host) interview author Steven Kotler around the time of the 2014 Winter Olympics in Sochi, Russia.

https://www.youtube.com/watch?v=Xt9xN9k3SCE

Steven Kotler's basic argument was that at the physical level, the elite athletes were basically the same, and those athletes best able to get into the flow state, and stay there for the duration of the contest had the advantage.

The basic premise of Kotler's book, *The Rise of Superman* is that there is a (highly elusive) state of being (an optimal state of body-brain combination) called the flow state. Two characteristics consistently associated with flow are (1) It always feels good: It is always a positive experience, and (2) It functions as a performance enhancer. Kotler even describes flow as being "The telephone booth where Clark Kent changes clothes, the place from where Superman emerges."

Here is Steven Kotler's talk at Google, "The Rise of Superman: Decoding the Science of Ultimate Human Performance".

https://www.youtube.com/watch?v=y1MHyyWsMeE

I have edited Kotler's exact spoken words for reading clarity and brevity.

When I was 30 years old, I got Lyme's disease. I spent the better portion of three years in bed. It's like having the worst flu crossed with paranoid schizophrenia. By the end of this, the doctors had pulled me off medicines. My stomach lining was bleeding out. There was nothing else they could do for me. I was functional 5–10% of the time. My mind was totally shut down. My body was in so much pain I could barely walk. I was hallucinating. My short-term memory was gone. My long-term memory was gone. It was all gone. At this point I was going to kill myself out of practicality. The only thing I was going to be from here on out was a burden to my friends and family. It was really a question of "when" and not "if" at that point.

In the middle of all this negative thinking a friend of mine showed up at my house and demanded that we go surfing. ... And she was insistent, wouldn't leave and kept badgering me. And finally I agreed, thinking, "What is the worst that can happen?" ... They took me out, helped me out, and gave me a big board. After about 30 seconds a wave came ... and I paddled into it ... and popped up into a completely different dimension. My senses were incredibly acute. I was clear-headed for the first time in years. ... The most incredible thing was that I felt great. I felt alive. The first wave felt good. I caught four more waves. After five waves, I was gone. They had to take me home. For 14 days I couldn't walk again. On the 15th day I went back to the ocean and I did it again. Again it felt great.

The cycle kept repeating itself. Over six months' time, I went from about 10% functionality to about 80% functionality. My first question was, "What the hell is going on? Surfing is not a cure for the auto-immune condition." Second, "I am a science writer by profession," so this led me to find out what was going on with me.

I strongly recommend that you plan to watch this entire talk. Allow for 75 minutes.

For me, this story is even more amazing than Joshua Foer winning the USA memory championship.

If you are interested, here are a couple of links, one to an HBR article by the author, and the other to some Flow-related videos.

http://blogs.hbr.org/2014/05/create-a-work-environment-that-fosters-flow/

http://riseofsuperman.com/videos/

Just like there are USA and World memory championship events, there is a Toastmasters World Championship of Public Speaking contest held every year. It is probably not a well-known contest except in public speaking, storytelling, and Toastmasters circles. I have studied DVDs of many of these contests, and have read some "How to Win the Championship" type of books on this subject. Now, I cannot help but wonder, if what was really going on at the level of neurobiology was that the winners (World Champions of Public Speaking) were better able to enter the flow state than the rest of the competition. It certainly seems to be an avenue worth investigating. I suspect flow states contributed significantly to victory in these annual contests. I suspect that future competitors best able to get into the flow state, while competing, may have a decided advantage.

I have been so taken up by this book, and the argument that deliberate practice in the flow state is the optimal route toward acquiring expertise, that I have made it one of my personal goals for PS&ST. My goal: I want to be able to enter the flow state each and every time I am public speaking or storytelling. In this state I will be most present, least distracted, best able to connect with my audience, best able to forget myself, and best able to serve my audience.

I recommend that you too make this one of your goals on your PS&ST voyage. "I will engage in deliberate practice in the flow state as much as I can. I will attempt to enter the flow state each and every time I am public speaking, presenting, or storytelling." This decision could be the one that contributes to your acquisition of expertise at double the rate of what was previously considered normal. This decision could be the one decision, more than any other, that transforms you into a selfless speaker. This decision could be the one that enables you to listen to and draw energy from your audiences more than any other.

One of my most basic mantras in PS&ST is "This is not about me." The flow state seems to be the ideal state to practice this mantra, because, as a matter of neurobiology, the parts within my brain that make "me" conscious of "me" are effectively shut down. In this state there is no differentiation (in cognition) between the speaker, the speech, and the audience.

So how does one get into this elusive flow state? According to Steven Kotler, one way is to know about flow triggers and surround oneself with as many of them as practical. He identifies 17 flow triggers, and separates them into four categories: external, internal, social, and creative.

What these triggers do is drive attention into the now, into the present, to the task at hand, and they shut out all other distractions and thoughts. This allows for maximum concentration and focus on the task at hand—and on nothing else. Many of our brain sub-systems that are normally (not-flow-state) "on" are effectively switched "off." These sub-systems, which normally make us aware of time, and aware of ourselves, go off-line. We no longer have any awareness, cognition, or consciousness of either time or ourselves.

If you remember from Csikszentmihalyi's TED Talk, (minutes 8–11) he says that we can process about 110 bits of information per second. The more of these 110 bits are devoted to the task at hand, the less are available for us to be conscious of ourselves, our bodies, time, etc. This, I will confess, makes a lot of sense to me.

Another characteristic of the flow state is that there is a massive release of multiple neurotransmitters. This makes us feel very good.

Therefore, in an effort to enter the flow state, one option is to surround ourselves with as many of these flow triggers as practical.

Another point the book makes is that the flow state is a part of a cycle; one which starts with (1) *struggle*, is followed by (2) *release*, which is then followed by (3) *flow,* and finally followed by (4) *recovery.*

When reading through the list of flow triggers, I couldn't help but notice that many of these conditions are present during PS&ST, making PS&ST a good opportunity to get into flow.

Here are the triggers as identified by Steven Kotler in his book, *The Rise of Superman*:

External: (1) Risk, (2) Rich environment, (3) Deep embodiment.

Internal: (4) Clear goals (more stress on clear, less stress on goals), (5) Immediate feedback, (6) Challenge/skills ratio.

Social: (7) Serious concentration, (8) Shared (clear) goals, (9) Good communication, (10) Equal participation, (11) Element of risk, (12) Familiarity (everyone knows everyone, all are on the same page, there is shared knowledge, there is a common language, communication is based on unspoken understandings), (13) Blending egos (collective humility, no one hogs the spotlight, everyone is involved), (14) A sense of control (a combination of autonomy and competence) (15) Close listening, (16) Always say YES (interactions should be additive, not argumentative. The goal is momentum, togetherness, and innovation from amplifying each other's ideas).

Creative: (17) Creativity is flow hack.

Let me comment a little more on point 6: challenge to skills ratio. It is sort of the same thing we read earlier in chapter 6. ("Talent is Overrated": *Noel Tichy, a professor at the University of Michigan business school and former chief of General Electric's famous Crotonville management development center uses a diagram of three concentric circles. He labels the inner circle "comfort circle," the middle one the "learning zone," and the outer one "panic zone."* **Only by choosing activities in the learning zone can one make progress. That's the location of skills and abilities that are just out of reach.** *We can never make progress in the comfort zone because these are activities we can already do easily, while the panic zone activities are so hard that we don't even know how to approach them.* **Identifying the learning zone, which is not simple, and then forcing oneself to stay continually in it as it changes, which is even harder**—*these are the first and most important characteristics of deliberate practice.)*

A key element is to set the challenge of the task at hand just outside the range of present skills. How much? About 4–5% more. This is the amount of stretch that requires full concentration, without anxiety leading to stress/panic, also called stretching without snapping. At this level of challenge the result is not certain. We may succeed, or we may not. We have to give the challenging task our best attention, and we are better able to receive immediate feedback, i.e. we are actively looking out for what is working and what is not working.

A fundamental difference between us (you and me) and elite athletes, is that elite athletes have become masters at identifying challenges that are +4% above current skills and training at that challenge level. The road to magic and extraordinary performance (and PS&ST expertise) is 4% + 4% + 4% + 4% + 4%, day after day, week after week, month after month and year after year. Self-knowledge is essential to knowing limits, and to setting 4% harder goals.

Now we are told that corporations are beginning to emulate the elite athlete approach. Here is something from the Google

Talk.

Major companies, including Microsoft, Ericsson, Patagonia and Toyota have realized that being able to control and harness this feeling of FLOW is the holy grail for any manager.

It seems serendipitous that PS&ST are surrounded by lots of these flow triggers. A reminder: The main benefit of a flow trigger is that it forces our attention back into the "now," into the present moment. Yes *FLOW* = No *Wandering Mind. Yes FLOW* = No *Awareness of Self or Ego. Yes FLOW* = No *(or dilated) Awareness of Time.* If after a presentation you wondered, "Where did all the time go?" you were probably in a low-grade flow state.

While we know that action adventure athletes have essentially become the best flow hackers on Earth, I suspect PM&Es are also decent flow hackers—after all, our professions place high demands on us. I can see, in my mind's eye, that PM&Es can, with planning, ingenuity, community, and new tech devices, take this to another level.

A pragmatic way to get to the flow state is to surround ourselves by as many of these flow triggers as we can. Let's investigate if these flow triggers are present, or can be made present while we engage in PS&ST.

Let's make a checklist of these triggers.

External

1. Risk—*certainly. There is risk associated anytime we PS&ST. We make ourselves vulnerable. We may miss an important point or connection between ideas that will reduce our professional credibility. We may stumble and stammer. We may make outright fools of ourselves. We may have a bout of stage fright. We may be asked questions we do not know the answers to. Yes there*

is risk each time we PS&ST, so we have this flow trigger in place—good.

2. Rich environment—*certainly. Any audience, small or large, that has focused its attention on us will capture our full attention. We have to pay attention—we cannot even imagine being distracted or drifting off. Yes there is a rich environment each time we PS&ST, so we have this flow trigger in place—good.*

3. Deep embodiment—*certainly. We discussed (in chapter 7) the various aspects of body sensations when the attention of a large group of people is directed on us. We may well feel some anxiety and some element of the fight-or-flight response: We cannot fully control this. We can use this to our benefit by recognizing "Good, these sensations in my body will force me to direct my attention into the now, to pay full attention to my audience, and will fortuitously help propel me further into flow." Yes there is a strong possibility of experiencing deep embodiment each time we PS&ST, so we likely have this flow trigger in place—good.*

Internal

4. Clear goals (with high stress on clear)—*certainly. If we do not have clear goals, it is 100% our own fault. Why are we even presenting without clear goals? Why would anyone do that? One more motivation for having clear goals is that they act as a flow trigger. For example, a clear goal of an icebreaker speech is to share myself; more specifically, my background, interests, and ambitions. One clear goal is that I want all of us to have final emotions and thoughts that we have a lot in common. Yes we can certainly ensure that we have clear goals in place each time we engage in public speaking and*

storytelling, so we have this flow trigger in place—good.

5. Immediate feedback—*certainly. One excellent reason to memorize a speech is that this frees us up to listen to and connect with the audience. Listening and connecting to an audience is to know what the audience is thinking and feeling. This is immediate feedback. Yes we can have an opportunity for immediate feedback each time we PS&ST, so we can have this flow trigger in place— good.*

6. Challenge / skills ratio—*certainly. We may have to work hard at this but it is achievable and, if we do not have this flow trigger in place, we can change that.*

Social

7. Serious concentration—*certainly.*
8. Shared (clear) goals— *hopefully.*
9. Good communication—*hopefully.*
10. Equal participation—*yes & no. A speech must sound conversational, but it is not a conversation. It can be a shared emotional rollercoaster ride, and it can be two-way flow of a positive energy. The more the audience feels like it is participating, (i.e. shares the speaker's emotions) the better—we have another flow trigger in place.*
11. Element of risk—*certainly.*
12. Familiarity (everyone knows everyone, all are on the same page, there is shared knowledge, there is a common language, communication is based on unspoken understandings)—*depends on venue and audience. It is worth noting that the more the familiarity, the better the chances of finding flow.*
13. Blending egos (collective humility, no one hogs the spotlight, everyone is involved)—*hopefully.*

14. A sense of control (a combination of autonomy and competence)—*achievable.*
15. Close listening—*achievable.*
16. Always say YES (interactions should be additive, not argumentative. The goal is momentum, togetherness, and innovation from amplifying each other's ideas)—*achievable.*

Creative

17. Creativity is flow hack.—*It depends.*

Yes, we have the opportunity to surround ourselves with a significant number of flow triggers. This is good.

How can we pragmatically proceed?

Take a look at Kotler's Google talk (minutes 35 to 42:30) and devise a plan made on this model. Taking a screenshot of the graphic at minute 35:22 may be useful to visualize and create a mind map for an entire speech project.

Struggle (beta brain waves: cortisol and norepinephrine) 36:15–38:00

For me, I see the speech preparation, or presentation preparation, phase as a struggle phase. There is researching, gathering of ideas, sources and stories, brainstorming, rewriting and mind mapping the script. There is usually doubt and occasionally despair. There may be time constraints. There is struggle when deciding on and constructing slides and other visual aids. There is struggle when deciding the staging of the delivery. There is struggle when practicing alone. There is struggle when receiving necessary feedback. Yes, there is certainly struggle associated with speech writing. This is good. We can appreciate the fact that this struggle is the pathway to flow. The more you struggle with the preparation, the better.

Reminder from Vikas Jhingran's book, *Emote*.

A speech when first conceived is rarely as beautiful as it ends up. Sometimes the final emotion, or the key idea is the only thing that remains from the original version.

The process of refining from the first draft to the final version of the speech is really where great speakers distinguish themselves.

Minute 36:15-38:00 of the Google talk is a good reminder of the struggle phase. The more of this we go through, the likelier we are to get into flow.

Release (alpha brain waves: nitric oxide) 38:00–38:45

In PS&ST, I equate this phase with pre-speech routines. Following some of my coaching with Sandra Zimmer, I began doing these routines diligently, as they were clearly working. So it was nice to find an explanation of sorts here—always makes the engineer in me happy. My pre-speech routines can be seen in Appendix 4. I suggest you experiment and have your own pre-speech routine in place—especially now that we know it is a part of the flow matrix. We can appreciate the fact that this release is on the pathway to flow. The better we can enter the release phase the more likely we are to find flow.

Flow (theta and gamma brain waves: dopamine, endorphins, anandamide) 38:45–40:30

We want to get into flow because it is always a positive experience and we are at our best. This is the ideal state to be in when giving a presentation. This is the Holy Grail. It is worth remembering that there are various levels of flow, so even getting into a low-grade flow state, for only a portion of your talk, is forward progress.

This is my *thirteenth wish* for you. May you eventually find flow every time you PS&ST.

Your audience will prefer to see you in flow. Period. One way to serve your audience is to be an expert at getting into the flow state.

Recovery (delta brain waves: serotonin, oxytocin) 40:30–42:30

Now that we know about this phase, it is important that we plan for it and allow it to do its work. I find the idea that this is where the consolidation of learning occurs, where the "just acquired higher skill" becomes the "new normal skill" to be fascinating. Without this phase we are not ready for the next +4% challenge.

This reminds me of something about running and exercising. Our muscles do not actually grow when running or exercise, rather they break down. It is only in the recovery stage between runs that the muscles rebuild and grow. I am guessing (and this is wild speculation on my part) that disciplined sleep routines, evangelized in chapter 6, also have a beneficial role in the consolidation of learning, in getting us to the "new normal."

I think that PM&Es will probably embrace this approach (finding flow as a holy grail when PS&ST) more than the rest of the world of PS&ST. There is elegance, science, planning, and benefit that the PM&E in me finds very appealing.

Flow is not so much PS&ST becoming easy, but it is PS&ST becoming easier. Flow is not so much PS&ST becoming totally rewarding, but it is PS&ST becoming more and more rewarding (more reward chemicals/neurotransmitters in circulation within our bodies). This is biology. Flow in PS&ST is not so much us becoming totally selfless, rather it is us becoming, as a matter of biology, less aware of our selves. Good enough for me!

Chapter 17

Our Closing Conversation

Dear reader, as we come to the end of the book, I cannot help but wonder—what is your final emotion? What are you feeling right now? What are you experiencing? Your final emotion will be the bedrock of your memory of this book. Not the content, not anything else. Your lasting memory of this book will likely be formed by how you felt during and immediately after your last interaction with this book—even if you did not make it to the end of the book.

I, for one, would never have had this realization had I not embarked on a PS&ST voyage a few years ago. This one realization alone can rewardingly change the way you plan and deliver your presentations. The vast majority of PM&Es are probably unaware of this approach, this option. This realization alone can have significant consequences for your relationships, your career and for our professions.

The way you and I are remembered by our colleagues, customers and others, very significantly depends on their final emotions at the end of their interactions with us. Think hard about this.

I believe that we PM&Es now have a propitiously timed opportunity to evangelize PS&ST, and in doing so become even more worthy ambassadors for our magnificent professions. Surely this can be a self-assigned part of our job descriptions.

I voiced these aspirations in the preface: *It is my hope that engineers and project managers increasingly communicate in a way that leaves everyone around them experiencing the same final emotion I felt at the end of the "Invictus" movie scene; inspired and committed to exceeding their own expectations.*

Deep down within you, don't you want to have the ability to communicate like this? I'm guessing we all do. The principles and tools of PS&ST are always available to us. Aren't they?

Will you join this initiative by committing to becoming an expert public speaker and storyteller? Will you join the small but growing ranks of PM&Es who are already evangelizing PS&ST within our workplaces and professions? Will you reach out to schools and colleges where PM&E is taught to the young and insist on a certain minimum standard of PS&ST expertise? Please at least consider it.

The era of *"Oh, PM&E is PM&E and PS&ST is PS&ST, and never the twain shall meet"* is surely a receding era, if not yet a bygone one. As surely as the era of *"Oh, East is East and West is West, and never the twain shall meet"* has passed, so too the thinking that PM&E and PS&ST are fundamentally unconnected shall pass.

It is my hope that someday in the not too distant future, PM&Es will routinely be thought of not only as smart and educated individuals, but as excellent public speakers and storytellers too ... PS&ST are lubricating oils that keep the machinery of engineering, project management, and relationship management running super smoothly. And engineers and project managers have moved, indeed pushed, the world forward as much or more than any other profession.

I recently finished reading Walter Isaacson's book, *The Innovators: How a Group of Hackers, Geniuses and Geeks Created the Digital Revolution.* I wholeheartedly recommend this book to any reader who loves or once loved engineering. It reminded me all over again, that yes indeed, engineers and project managers have moved the world forward as much or more than any other profession.

Sadly, the larger world scarcely knows or acknowledges the depth of this contribution. Sadly, the larger world scarcely knows how much joy and fulfillment we PM&Es have been blessed with, when making these mammoth contributions.

Reading this book made me feel the way I used to feel as a young engineer, when learning about and admiring—dare I say falling in love with—the engineering marvels of the marine engineering world. Human ingenuity is an endless source of inspiration. It is nothing short of magical.

In the last chapter of his book, Walter Isaacson writes: *Most of the successful innovators and entrepreneurs in this book had one thing in common: They were product people. They cared about, and deeply understood, the engineering and design. They were not primarily marketers or salesmen of financial types; when such folks took over companies, it was often to the detriment of sustained innovation. "When the sales guys run the company, the product guys don't matter so much, and a lot of them just turn off," Steve Jobs said. Larry Page felt the same: "The best leaders are those with the deepest understanding of the engineering and product design."*

I would expand this last statement a bit: "The best leaders are those with the deepest understanding of the engineering and product design, with outstanding execution (i.e. project management) prowess—and who have either a 'good-enough' competency, or flat-out excellence, in PS&ST."

I truly believe that if product teams do not wish to cede power to sales teams, acquiring expertise (starting in college) in PS&ST is one of the best ways of preventing this from happening. The sales teams are undoubtedly better trained in PS&ST and consequently win more arguments. This situation is easily correctable. I have heard the famous public speaker Craig Valentine pose this question, *"Are you in your way, or are you on your way?"* It's a valid question, isn't it? Are we, PM&Es, in our own way when we inflexibly deny or ignore the necessity of PS&ST expertise? You get to decide this one for yourself.

This closing conversation would be incomplete without acknowledging the potentially dark side of PS&ST expertise. Expert public speakers and storytellers have the ability to mesmerize audiences. Period. It is irresponsible, even foolhardy, to stubbornly and endlessly deny this. Expert public speakers and storytellers can energize a crowd and propel it to action—even if that action is against our individual values and best judgment. This should not be underestimated. Some of history's most horrific leaders were outstanding orators. It is our responsibility to remain idealists without illusions—no one else's. When listening to any speaker or storyteller, par excellence, I counsel you to keep this thought somewhere in the back of your mind, "An expert public speaker and storyteller with selfish incentives, mal-intent, or flat-out malevolence is a very bad combination indeed." The principle of "caveat emptor" or "buyer beware" applies. Enough said.

We have voyaged through the basics of PS&ST. I thank you for sharing the journey. If you still have not decided to dive in and acquire PS&ST expertise, then I have failed in my primary objective. I will not pretend otherwise. A simple question for you please, "Are you on your way, or are you in your way?"

I reiterate my basic argument one final time. Deciding (really and truly 100% deciding) to become an expert PS&ST is probably harder than actually becoming an expert public speaker and storyteller. Once you make the decision, a 100% commitment, action, and growth will inevitably follow, especially if you have put together a good multi-year project plan and have the support of those around you.

About three years ago a man visited one of my Toastmasters clubs. He was a seasoned, successful professional entertainer, who had won several entertainment awards. He was confident in himself, comfortable on stage, and wanted to polish and practice a particular presentation that he had been presenting to his audiences for years. He is a great guy and a fabulous contributor to our club. Once he joined our club he dove right into the communication and leadership programs. He practiced regularly, took on leadership roles and simultaneously improved his 45-minute professional lecture—his New Year's resolution. His wife Carol Ann, then a director in one of the largest hospital systems in Houston, was protective of her husband's prized lecture material. She came in one evening to hear a five-minute excerpt of his speech. She was pleasantly surprised with the accurate and kind evaluation he received. She was especially impressed with the suggestions for improvement, which were both detailed and encouraging. Her husband's work was enhanced by the evaluation. Intrigued, she continued to accompany him as a guest. We often asked her to participate and occasionally she took on a (non-speaking) meeting role, like timekeeper. She, however, refused any and all speaking opportunities. I spoke with her regularly and judged her to be a very decent, friendly, and competent lady—and a delightful conversationalist. She came to our meetings faithfully every Monday evening for six months, and was always willing to help with non-speaking roles.

One evening due to the absence of one of our members, I asked her to take on his speaking role, as we really needed her help. This time something in her clicked—without hesitation, she obliged. She spoke! After the meeting, I suggested she consider joining our club. She was hesitant again, but this time said, "Yes."

A few years later she told me how hard it had been for her to finally decide to join. I had no idea that to her, public speaking was so intimidating. In her own words: *"It took six MONTHS for me to go from a guest in the audience to approaching the lectern for the first time. Yes, the Toastmaster members were friendly and yes I could carry on a great conversation with them BEFORE and AFTER the meeting, however, up there on that stage, behind the lectern I thought I would fall apart! It was more frightening than anything I had ever felt as an adult! My heart pounded in my chest till I thought it was going to burst! I could feel my face go red. My mouth was dry; my palms were wet. I couldn't remember anything. My mind drew complete blanks! I felt like I was going to pass out, and when I didn't, I wished I had! By the time I finally made it to the lectern for the first time, I thought they would have to call me an ambulance!"*

She now laughs and tells this story occasionally to our new and frightened members and guests. It is compelling, authentic, and has inspired others around her. She adds: *"It is like playing the piano; to become successful is to practice and fail, practice and fail—then one day when you don't even notice it, you are "on your way." Without even realizing it, you are the confident speaker and leader that you saw in other people. This continues to be an awesome journey—Yes! I am on my way, as a Toastmaster friend of mine just recently told me, and I now believe him!"*

I had no idea Carol Ann had to battle this much anxiety, but battle it she did, and overcome it she did. Today she is an advanced, engaging, and creative speaker. Today she is a confident and much better leader. I suspect she always had these attributes in her but Toastmasters brought these things to the surface, where she is able to use them. She is a shining star example of the transformative power that PS&ST has to change us.

She is making the same point that I am—Just Get Started!

Mark Brown, a hugely respected and admired past Toastmasters International world champion of public speaking has frequently said, "Your life tells a story and there's someone out there that needs to hear it." This is true.

Dear reader: Your life too tells a story and there is someone out there who needs to hear it.

Dear reader: If deep down you know the fear of public speaking is your primary issue, then there is a world of help and support available to you. Get the hard work of deciding and committing to PS&ST expertise out of the way. Good things will follow.

Dear reader: If you are amongst the more fortunate like me, and are not really constrained by glossophobia, then what are you waiting for? We need you to be an ambassador for our professions. We need you to evangelize PS&ST to those who are yet to join our great professions. We need you to tell your story because there are young, embryonic PM&Es who need to hear it.

Good luck on the voyages ahead! May you be blessed with fair winds and following seas.

I know in a way that is non-negotiable ... we are all in the same boat; together.

And one way or another, now and always, my wish for each and every one of you, indeed for everyone on our planet is this, "May God Bless You, and All Who Sail With You."

Oh ... one final thought.

Many years ago the great British explorer George Mallory ... who was to die on Mount Everest ... was asked why did he want to climb it. He said ... "Because it is there."

Well ... PS&ST is there ... and together, PM&Es, we're going to climb it ... and new horizons are there ... and they beckon. And ... therefore ... as we set sail ... we ask God's blessing ... on what could be the most exhilarating and frightening ... even greatest adventure on which we ever embark.

Appendices

Appendix 1: Exercises to Complete

Exercises #1: Page 16: Write your own life story in no less than 5,000 words.

Exercise #2: Page 33: Start a story file, a failure file, and a life timeline.

Exercise (optional): Page 41: Convert my deliberately long life story into a 6-minute speech.

Exercise #3: Page 61: Make your project charter.

Exercise #4: Page 83: Select a portion of the JFK speech and practice aloud, standing-up, using the Churchill/ Roosevelt/Reagan method.

Exercise #5: Page 86: Practice the selected section of the Hillary Clinton speech aloud, standing-up, using the Churchill/ Roosevelt/Reagan method.

Exercise #6: Page 94: Take a few speeches and insert these words, as applicable/appropriate

Comment: Do this with your speeches, famous speeches, TED Talks, political speeches, humorous speeches, corporate presentations, etc.

Exercise #7: Page 134: Say this aloud. So what if you look or feel stupid? Say it anyway. "Fear is a familiar friend—always reminding me to give my best. To give anything less than my best … is to sacrifice my gifts."

Exercise #8: Page 146: Check out the endings of one of your past speeches and any other speech that you like. Try to determine and envision the final emotion the audience was/will be left with.

Exercise #9: Page 168: Select three to five speeches and then analyze how well the opening was crafted.

Exercise #10: Page 203: When listening to the news, or a speech, try speaking along with the broadcaster or speaker and listen for the difference in your vocal variety.

Exercise #11: Page 203: When watching famous speeches, occasionally shut off the sound and pay attention to gestures, stage movement, and body language. Then compare these to a video recording of one of your presentations.

Exercise #12: Page 216: Say this using your name as often as necessary. Till you get it. "I, Rashid N. Kapadia am in speaking, therefore I Rashid N. Kapadia am in sales."

Exercise #13: Page 217: Convert your written life story into an icebreaker speech.

Appendix 2: Books and Products Worth Buying

My acceptance criteria for a book or product recommendation is a "yes" answer to all four of the following questions:

1. Will the referred product or book add value at a fair price to my customer, the reader?
2. Will the referred product or book make my customer a better PS&ST? Assuming of course that you use it or read it diligently.
3. Do I wish I had this product or book at the very start of my PS&ST voyage?
4. Do I now own this recommended product or book?

Prices for most books are for indication only. Prices from Amazon website in November 2014.

Total Cost for buying all books and HBR articles—US $ 700

Total Cost for buying recommended products—US $ 430

Preface

Playing the Enemy: Nelson Mandela and the Game that Made a Nation: John Carlin (US $13)

Emote: Using Emotions to Make Your Message Memorable: Vikas Jhingran (US $12)

How to Read a Book: The Classic Guide to Intelligent Reading: Mortimer J. Adler and Charles Van Doren. (US $11)

Chapter 1: Who Am I?

Profiles in Courage: John F. Kennedy (US $12)

Speak Like Churchill, Stand Like Lincoln: 21 Powerful Secrets of History's Greatest Speakers: James C. Hume (US $13)

Long Walk to Freedom: The Autobiography of Nelson Mandela: Nelson Mandela (US $11)

Chapter 2: Who Are You?

It's Your Time to Shine: How to Overcome Fear of Public Speaking, Develop Authentic Presence and Speak from Your Heart: Sandra Zimmer (US $17)

Chapter 3: Your Project Charter

APE: Author, Publisher, Entrepreneur: How to Publish a Book: Guy Kawasaki and Shawn Welch (US $19)

Chapter 4: To the Moon ... and ... To the Stars Beyond

Speak Like Churchill, Stand Like Lincoln: 21 Powerful Secrets of History's Greatest Speakers: James C Hume (priced in Chapter 1)

The Brain and Emotional Intelligence: New Insights: Daniel Goleman (US $10)

Chapter 5: Basic Parts of a Speech

Toastmasters International: Competent Communication Manual: A Practical Guide to Becoming a Better Speaker (Member Price US $8)

Steve Jobs: Walter Isaacson (US $20)

Harvard Business Review: How to Give a Killer Presentation: Lessons from TED: Chris Anderson: June 2013 REPRINT R1306K: (HBR website US $9)

12 Ways to Become a Speaking Star: What Hollywood Can Teach You about Great Presentation Skills: Patricia Fripp. (US $3 e-book only)

Chapter 6: The Fittest Speaker, The Expert Speaker

HBR: "Why We Humblebrag About Being Busy": Greg McKeown

The Willpower Instinct: How Self-Control Works, Why It Matters, and What You Can Do to Get More of It: Kelly McGonigal (US $12)

What I Talk About When I Talk About Running: Haruki

Murakami (US $10)

Making of an Expert: K. Anders Ericsson, Michael J. Prietula, Edward T. Cokely HBR Prod. #: R0707J-PDF-ENG: (US $9)

Bounce: Mozart, Federer, Picasso, Beckham, and the Science of Success: Matthew Syed (US $13)

Talent is Overrated: What Really Separates World Class Performers from Everybody Else: Geoff Colvin (US $10)

Outliers: The Story of Success: Malcolm Gladwell (US $10)

Drive: The Surprising Truth About What Motivates Us: Daniel Pink (US $11)

The Rise of Superman: Decoding the Science of Ultimate Human Performance: Steven Kotler (US $18)

Chapter 7: The Fear of Public Speaking

It's Your Time to Shine: How to Overcome Fear of Public Speaking, Develop Authentic Presence and Speak from Your Heart: Sandra Zimmer (priced in Chapter 2)

The Book of Lists: 1977: David Wallechinsky, Irving Wallace, Amy Wallace (not recommended for buying— included here because it has been referenced in this chapter)

The Willpower Instinct: How Self-Control Works, Why It Matters, and What You Can Do to Get More of It: Kelly McGonigal (priced in Chapter 6)

Chapter 8: Ending Your Speech

Emote: Using Emotions to Make Your Message Memorable: Vikas Jhingran (priced in Preface)

Social Intelligence: The New Science of Human Relationships: Daniel Goleman (US $10)

Toastmasters International: Concluding Your Speech: Digital Item 271 DCD (Free to members of Toastmasters)

Chapter 9: Leaders Are Speakers (Rondo 1)

None

Chapter 10: Opening Your Speech
Toastmasters International: "Beginning Your Speech" Digital Item: 270 DCD (Free to members of Toastmasters)

Chapter 11: Another Copernican Revolution? (Rondo 2)
The Happiness Advantage: The Seven Principles of Positive Psychology that Fuel Success and Performance at Work: Shawn Achor (US $17)

Chapter 12: Storytelling
TATA Log: Eight Modern Stories from a Timeless Institution: Harish Bhat ($7, Kindle version)
The Art of War: Sun Tzu (US $10)
Whoever Tells the Best Story Wins: How to Use Your Own Stories to Communicate With Power and Impact: Annette Simmons (US $17)
The Leader's Guide to Storytelling: Mastering the Art & Discipline of Business Narrative: Steven Denning (US $23)
Strategic Storytelling: How to Create Persuasive Business Presentations: Dave McKinsey (US $20)
Product: Edge of Their Seats Storytelling Home Study Course for Speakers: How to Keep Your Audiences Riveted, Revved Up and Ready for Your Message: Craig Valentine: 6 CD set. (US $300)

Chapter 13: Orthodox PS&ST Competencies
The Art of War: Sun Tzu (priced in Chapter 12)
Toastmasters International: "Your Speaking Voice": (Free to members of Toastmasters)
To Move the World: JFK's Quest for Peace: Jeffrey Sachs: (US $20)
Toastmasters International: "Gestures: Your Body Speaks" (Free to members of Toastmasters)
The Pin Drop Principle: Captivate, Influence and Communicate

Better Using the Time-Tested Methods of Professional Performers: David Lewis & G. Riley Mills (US $19)

Stand-Up Comedy: The Book: Judy Carter (US $14)

Product: Laff Pack: Darren LaCroix (combination of audio lessons, DVDs and a book; US $130)

10 Simple Secrets of the World's Greatest Business Communicators: Carmine Gallo (US $13)

Pitch Perfect: How To Say It Right the First Time, Every Time: Bill McGowan and Alisa Bowman (US $21)

Speaker, Leader, Champion: Succeed at Work Through the Power of Public Speaking: Jeremy Donovan and Ryan Avery (US $14)

The Presentation Secrets of Steve Jobs: How to Be Insanely Great in Front of Any Audience: Carmine Gallo (US $16)

Lend Me Your Ears: All You Need To Know About Making Speeches and Presentations: Max Atkinson (US $28)

Speak Like Churchill, Stand Like Lincoln: 21 Powerful Secrets of History's Greatest Speakers: James C Hume (priced in Chapter 1)

Say It Like Obama and Win: The Power of Speaking With Purpose and Vision: Shel Leanne (US $19)

How to Deliver a TED Talk: Secrets of the World's Most Inspiring Presentations: Jeremy Donovan (US $15)

Talk Like TED: The 9 Public-Speaking Secrets of the World's Top Minds: Carmine Gallo (US $16)

How To Win the Toastmasters World Championship of Public Speaking: 2012 International Speech Contest: Jeremy Donovan (US $10)

World Class Speaking in Action: 50 Certified World Class Coaches Show You How To Present, Persuade, and Profit: Craig Valentine and Mitch Meyer (US $16)

Chapter 14: Creating the Icebreaker Speech

The Alliance: Managing Talent in the Networked Age: Reid Hoffman, Ben Casnocha & Chris Yeh (US $15)

The Great Work of Your Life: A Guide for the Journey to Your True Calling: Stephen Cope (US $18)

Keep Your Eyes on the Prize: An Exercise in Life Purpose, Random Acts of Kindness and Generosity: Frederick Pearce and Angela Christensen (US $11)

The Values Factor: The Secret to Creating an Inspired and Fulfilling Life: Dr. John Demartini (US $12) *Harvard Business Review: How to Give a Killer Presentation:*

Lessons from TED: Chris Anderson June 2013 REPRINT R1306K: (priced in Chapter 2)

Emote: Using Emotions to Make Your Message Memorable: Vikas Jhingran (priced in Preface)

Whoever Tells the Best Story Wins: How to Use Your Own Stories to Communicate With Power and Impact: Annette Simmons priced in chapter 12)

Chapter 15: Memorizing, Listening, and Connecting

Moonwalking With Einstein: The Art and Science of Remembering Everything: Joshua Foer (US $10)

Search Inside Yourself: The Unexpected Path to Achieving Success, Happiness (and World Peace): Chade-Meng Tan (US $13)

Be Heard Now! Tap into Your Inner Speaker and Communicate with Ease: Lee Glickstein (US $16)

Chapter 16: Finding Flow in Public Speaking and Storytelling

Flow: The Psychology of Optimal Experience: Mihaly Csikszentmihalyi (Kindle e-book US $8.99)

The Rise of Superman: Decoding the Science of Ultimate Human Performance: Steven Kotler (priced in Chapter 6)

HBR: "Create a Work Environment That Fosters Flow": Steven Kotler

Chapter 17: Our Closing Conversation

The Innovators: How a Group of Hackers, Geniuses and Geeks Created the Digital Revolution: Walter Isaacson (US $21)

Appendix 3: My Wishes for You

Consider using this as a checklist to see if you are staying on track

First: Page 17: May you always have a wonderfully rounded and upwardly-mobile-professional-life!

Second: Page 34: Someday, may your career-changing stories, publically delivered, be as enchanting, entertaining, motivating, and inspiring as Craig Valentine's.

Third: Page 63: May you always be a successful project manager, executing all your projects in scope, on time, and within budget. And with top quality.

Fourth: Page 70: As you set sail on your PS&ST voyage, may you be blessed with fair winds and following seas.

Fifth: Page 85: When it comes your time to masterfully combine soaring rhetoric with pragmatism: May you always do it right, may you do it first, and most of all, may you always be bold!

Sixth: Page 98: May you someday give at least one unforgettable, artful, and minimal talk; with the simplicity, purity, charm, and grace of the Stanford June 2005 commencement.

Seventh: Page 110: I hope you find a coach who convinces you, "You may not be the most talented person in the world ... but you sure as hell can be the fittest."

Eighth: Page 134: May you always see the very natural fear of public speaking for what it is: An Inevitable Bridge; not an Impregnable Wall.

Ninth: Page 149: May all your speech and presentation closings generate total neural resonance.

Tenth: Page 170: May your openings be bold, may they capture your audiences' attention and good will, and may they rapidly generate neural resonance.

Eleventh: Page 236: May your icebreaker speech be one,

which your entire family is proud of, and one, which has the potential to rapidly build trust.

Twelfth: Page 250: May your PS&ST voyage culminate in you becoming an expert memorizer, an expert listener, an expert connector, and an expert at generating neural resonance.

Thirteenth: Page 263: May you eventually find flow every time you engage in PS&ST.

Finally: Page 272: May God Bless You, and All Who Sail With You.

With Warm Regards

Rashid

Appendix 4: My Pre-Speech Preparation

These notes have been compiled over many years. They work for me. They will probably not work the same for you. Make your own notes. Take all the time you need.

- Get a full eight hours of sleep.
- Exercise in the morning—include some vigorous / interval type of training.
- Express (and experience in my body) gratitude for the opportunity to speak.
- Engage in some type of full body movement for one to three minutes every hour.
- Engage in deep, slow breathing of three to five breaths per minute every hour: one to two minutes every hour or every two hours. Focus only on breath.
- Do short full body scans: Direct positive energy to parts that are struggling.
- Hold no negative energy or thoughts!
- Participate in a meditation or attention-training routine for 15–30 minutes.
- Have a grounding exercise.
- Check that my equipment, notes, visual aids, etc., are all properly packed, tested, and ready to go.

Read some of Sandra Zimmer's Book *Your Time to Shine* highlights (from location 1235 onward).

Engage in a grounding exercise—complete 15 minutes, with audio.

Just before starting speaking:

1. Ground
2. Connect with and internally describe/acknowledge my

inner feelings/climate
3. Make connection with audience.

While speaking:
1. Receive my "audience" and reduce focus on the "performance" aspect.
2. Master the skill of taking in my audience (and the world in general) with soft eyes.

Location 1467: Before any presentation, make a commitment to love my audience. Silently say to myself, "I am here to love you and share myself with you." This simple declaration of loving others automatically changes my feelings toward them. It changes my chemistry—and my internal climate.

Location 1475: Establish a mindset of service. Before any talk, remind myself that I am here to be of service, to share what I know and to let go of the outcome. Say this phrase over and over again in my mind, "I am here to love you and to share myself with you."

From location 1872
Silent Connection
First element of opening is silent connection. Before you ever open your mouth to say a word, the most important thing to do is to make connection with yourself and with your audience. Use the first few seconds of your presentation to establish a two-way connection with your listeners.

3 Steps
1. First, as you take your place as the center of attention, breathe and ground. Take 5 to 10 seconds to establish your presence in the space. Plant your feet on the ground,

with feet firmly planted one to two feet apart. Drop energy down into your feet to ground yourself in that place. Take a couple of deep breaths that are deeply rooted in your ribcage.

2. Second, turn your attention inside yourself. Tune in to how you feel to be standing as the center of attention. Identify a word or phrase that describes how you truly feel in this moment. You cannot plan it, because you don't know how you will be until you are standing at the center of attention. Whatever the feeling is, be honest with yourself and give yourself the permission to experience it.

Focus your attention on your true feelings (do not avoid this step) for only a few seconds to connect to your true self. If you want to connect to others, you must first connect to yourself.

3. Contact your audience. Once you have connected to your insides, look around the room at the individuals in your audience to see who is there. Land your eyes gently upon several people in the audience, using soft eye connection to receive each person you contact. Take in the energy of love and support from individuals in the group. Give yourself enough time to really feel the sense of energy coming to you from each person.

How Simon Sinek Delivered His TED Talk: No matter the size of the audience, I think of them as my closest friends. I have a mantra that I say out loud before I go on stage, "You're here to give. You're here to share."

Lee Glickstein "Be Heard Now"

It's all about Relational Presence.

We have to forget about being good, and remember to be ourselves.

They do not care what you know until they know that you care.

The key to connecting with any audience is not knowing how to give to them—but knowing how to receive support from them.

Message is important—but the depth of our commitment to that message, and our relationship with our audience, is even more important.

Develop capacity to listen while speaking, to both my audience and myself. Key element of success is listening with no agenda. Listen attentively with soft and available eyes.

It is our receptivity that draws people to us.

Energy going out and energy coming in are both really the same ... it is connection.

3 x Basic Steps to Connecting with any Audience (page 97)

1. Stand with your feet planted into the center of the earth—and listen to your audience before you begin speaking.
2. Speak clearly, from the heart, in short sentences. Say every sentence into the eyes and heart of a human being in the audience.
3. Spend 5–10 seconds of quality time with each listener before moving on to another.

4 x Questions the Audience has for you. *Answer these questions.*

1. Who are you? (page 180)

2. Why are you here?
3. What are we going to do?
4. What's in it for me?

Craig Valentine

Pre-Game for Public Speaking (Pre-speech Rituals)

Ritual One (60 minutes to go): Warm up your voice.

Make sure your voice is ready and resonant and clear. Hold a note for a few seconds, taking a breath, and then switch to a higher note. After each breath, hold a higher and higher note. Make sure to speak from the diaphragm rather than the throat.

Ritual Two (45 minutes to go): While you're up on stage, this is a good time to go over your opening lines one more time. Once you have your opening down cold, you'll feel much more confident about the rest of your speech. Remember, you must come out with a bang not with a whimper.

Ritual Three (10-15 minutes to go): As your audience members start filling in the seats, mentally send them good thoughts. Really look at each of them. For example, I usually think, "I hope you get what you need to lift your life to another level." Or I simply think, "I'm glad you're here, and I hope you get more than you expected from this program." The key to sending them good thoughts is that it once again forces you to go where most speakers never go. Many speakers worry about themselves before they take the stage. The most effective speakers think about their audience.

Ritual Four (2-10 minutes to go): You'll need one final way to ground yourself and get your energy high so that the best of you comes forward to serve your audience. Use a song, (first minute from theme of Remember the Titans) photograph, good thoughts—good words—good deeds, or something similar.

Last thing to say to myself before taking the stage.

"Please help me forget myself, remember my speech, and touch my audience in a wonderfully positive and impactful way."

Darren LaCroix—Connect DVD

4 Questions to ask five minutes before speaking
1. What is my intent?
2. Am I present?
3. Will I have fun?
4. How would I give this presentation if it were my last one ever?

AT THE EVENT (one hour to five minutes before)
1. Sit in the four corners of the room and see what the audience will see.
2. Q&A before the speech.
3. Shake hands and say hello.
4. Connect to yourself.

The Pin Drop Principle: Captivate, Influence & Communicate Better Using the Time-Tested Methods of Professional Performers—David Lewis & G. Riley Mills

5-Minute Physical Warm-Up
This is what actors do to warm up before performing/ acting.

Shortly before I go before my audience, take five minutes to loosen and warm up my body.

1. Neck: Let my head fall forward and stretch the neck muscles. Next, rotate my left ear to my left shoulder and my right ear to my right shoulder.
2. Eyes: Alternate from squinting (little eyes) to wide-eyed (big eyes).
3. Face: Alternate between my biggest expression (surprise) to my smallest expression (sour) to engage the muscles of the face.
4. Tongue: Stretch my tongue to my nose, my chin, and my cheeks.
5. Lips: Blow air through my lips to make a motorboat sound.
6. Jaw: Mimic chewing a very large piece of bubblegum to stretch the jaw muscles.
7. Shoulders: Roll shoulders in a circular motion. Then reverse the direction. Shrug and release.
8. Arms: Extend my arms and rotate them in a circular motion. Reverse.
9. Wrists: Rotate my wrists in a circular motion. Reverse.
10. Fingers: As if my fingers are dripping with water, vigorously shake them dry.
11. Back: Mimic the motion of hugging a tree to stretch out the back muscles.
12. Chest: Mimic the motion of crushing an orange between my shoulder blades to stretch out my chest.
13. Legs: Shake out any tension in my legs. Follow with deep knee bends.
14. Ankles: Standing on one foot, rotate my lifted ankle in circular motion. Repeat while standing on other foot.

The Pin Drop Principle: Captivate, Influence & Communicate Better Using the Time-Tested Methods of Professional Performers—David Lewis & G. Riley Mills

Home Base Position

Stay in this position for three to five minutes while meditating (i.e. meditating while standing up).

1. Stand with my feet shoulder-width apart and my weight evenly distributed.
2. Make sure my knees are unlocked.
3. Center and lock my pelvis to avoid shifting and swaying.
4. Let my arms, hands and fingers relax by my sides.
5. Hold my chest open and elevated.
6. Keep my shoulders relaxed.
7. Keep my chin parallel to the ground.
8. Focus my eyes forward.
9. Imagine that I have a string coming straight out of the top of my head, and someone is gently pulling on it.

Bounce: Mozart, Federer, Picasso, Beckham and the Science of Success: Matthew Syed. Page 218. Location 2221

I worked with three leading sports psychologists over ten years, and by the end of that period, I had my mental preparation down to a fine art. Precisely 15 minutes before a match was scheduled to begin, and having already warmed up, got the feel of my paddle in the practice hall, and talked tactics with my coach, I would vanish out of the hall and make my way over to my carefully chosen retreat.

Once there, in quiet and solitude, I would close my eyes

and begin a carefully rehearsed sequence of deep breathing. Inhale, relax; inhaaale relaaax; inhaaaaaale relaaaaaax. When one is first starting out it can take a few good minutes to quieten one's mind, but after long practice it took me only 90 seconds or so to get my heart rate down and my mind into a state of deep relaxation.

With my mind nice and quiet, I would begin a process of what psychologists call positive imagery; in my case a series of vivid recollections of the greatest and most inspiring table tennis matches I have ever played. First I would be looking in from the outside, like a spectator seeing the marvelous strokes, applauding the audacious attacks, marveling at the array and diversity of skills.

Then the perspective would switch, and I would be inhabiting my own body, feeling the sensuousness of the ball on the paddle, the uninhibited flow of my movement, and the exhilaration of playing to the best of my ability and beyond. Then I'd switch focus and imagine myself playing my upcoming opponent, executing the tactics discussed with my coach and sensing a deep and growing feeling of optimism.

I can feel my confidence solidifying. I can feel my doubts dissolving. I am feeling better and better.

Then another mental switch to what psychologists called "positive affirmations." I am no longer seeing myself in action, but stating the following, strangely powerful words "You can win." Over and over. With growing conviction. Note that I am not saying: "I can win." I am talking to my inner self, as if trying to talk him out of his default skepticism. The last few affirmations are ever so slightly different: "You WILL win! You WILL win!"

And with that, I open my eyes, my head actually nodding in agreement, my faced etched with conviction, my lips smiling. Slowly I walk back to the competition arena, nod at my coach, exchange a high five, and walk onto court to shake hands with my opponent. I am in precisely the place, mentally, I want to be. I am one with myself and the world.

Appendix 5: Links/URLs

Preface
Invictus: We need inspiration ...
https://www.youtube.com/watch?v=TQhns5AwAkA

NASA: 100+ Lessons Learned for Project Managers (lesson no. 78)
http://www.nasa.gov/offices/oce/llis/imported_content/lesson_1956.html

Chapter 1: Who Am I?
Craig Valentine's website: see video on the home page.
http://www.craigvalentine.com/
https://www.youtube.com/watch?v=obS8KY9zY-MA&list=PLOUOKnL3iJ6CleE8bU6hmF9XfGPnSbMfb

Read / Bookstore story: story #20: encouragement to read forever
http://www.craigvalentine.com/20storiestall

Chapter 2: Who are You?
None

Chapter 3: Your Project Charter
The Moth: http://themoth.org

Chapter 4: To the Moon ... and ... To the Stars Beyond
Rice University "We choose to go to the moon" speech (http://er.jsc.nasa.gov/seh/ricetalk.htm

American Rhetoric: Top 100 Speeches. Hillary Clinton.
http://www.americanrhetoric.com/speeches

hillary-clintonbeijingspeech.htm

Chapter 5: Basic Parts of a Speech

Steve Jobs: "How to live before you die"
http://www.ted.com/talks/steve_jobs_how_to_live_
before_you_die

Steve Jobs Stanford Commencement Address 2005
Analysis: Eleonora Pinto
http://prezi.com/4cafnh0joxk4/steve-jobs-
stanford-commencement-address-2005-analysis

Mind Map of Steve Jobs Stanford Commencement
Address: Nathan Chitty
https://www.youtube.com/watch?v=Ul4eI0bQccQ

HBR: How to Give a Killer Presentation
https://hbr.org/2013/06/how-to-give-a-killer-
presentation

Chapter 6: The Fittest Speaker, The Expert Speaker

TED: Arianna Huffington: "How to succeed? Get more
sleep."
http://www.ted.com/talks/arianna_huffington_how_to_
succeed_get_more_sleep#t-54943

TED: Jessa Gamble: "Our natural sleep cycle"
http://www.ted.com/talks/jessa_gamble_how_to_sleep/
transcript?language=en

TED: Russell Foster: "Why do we sleep?"
http://www.ted.com/talks/russell_foster_why_do_we_
sleep

TED: Jeff Iliff: "One more reason to get a good night's sleep"
http://www.ted.com/talks/jeff_iliff_one_more_reason_to_get_a_good_night_s_sleep

HBR: "Why We Humblebrag About Being Busy," by Greg McKeown
http://blogs.hbr.org/2014/06/why-we-humblebrag-about-being-busy

TED: Christopher McDougall: "Are we born to run?"
http://www.ted.com/talks/christopher_mcdougall_are_we_born_to_run

TED: May El-Khalil: "Making peace is a marathon"
http://www.ted.com/talks/may_el_khalil_making_peace_is_a_marathon

"101-year-old Fauja Singh runs the London Marathon"
https://www.youtube.com/watch?v=gCY0 Xx92YvQ

Chapter 7: The Fear of Public Speaking

TED: Megan Washington: "Why I live in mortal dread of public speaking"
http://www.ted.com/talks/megan_washington_why_i_live_in_mortal_dread_of_public_speaking

Sandra Zimmer: Self Expression Center: Videos.
http://www.self-expression.com/Free_Videos.shtml

TM Vision: Fear of Public Speaking: article.
http://tmvision.org/speaking/people-fear-public-speaking-death

TED Ed: Mikael Cho: "The science of stage fright (and how to overcome it)"
https://www.youtube.com/watch?v=K93fMnFKwfI
http://blog.ted.com/2013/10/16/required-watching-for-any-ted-speaker-the-science-of-stage-fright/comment-page-2

Psychology Today: "The Real Story of Risk" Article
http://www.psychologytoday.com/blog/the-real-story-risk/201211/the-thing-we-fear-more-death

TED: Amy Cuddy: "Your body language shapes who you are"
http://www.ted.com/talks/amy_cuddy_your_body_language_shapes_who_you_are

"Playing a musical instrument"
http://ed.ted.com/lessons/how-playing-an-instrument-benefits-your-brain-anita-collins

Chapter 8: Ending Your Speech
TED: Daniel Kahneman: "The riddle of experience vs. memory"
http://www.ted.com/talks/daniel_kahneman_the_riddle_of_experience_vs_memory?language=en

Vikas Jhingran: Various
https://www.youtube.com/watch?v=mDaOWYCkvvc
http://www.toastmasterspodcast.com/index.php/rss-feed/105-toastmasters-podcast-079-emote-with-2007-world-champion-of-public-speaking-vikas-jhingran

TED: Sting: "How I started writing songs again"
http://www.ted.com/talks/sting_how_i_started_writing_
songs_again?language=en

Ronald Reagan: The Space Shuttle Challenger Tragedy
Address
http://www.americanrhetoric.com/speeches/
ronaldreaganchallenger.htm
https://www.youtube.com/watch?v=Qa7icmqgsow

Nelson Mandela: Inaugural Address.
https://www.youtube.com/watch?v=grh03-NjHzc

Chapter 9: Leaders Are Speaker (Rondo 1)
Bloomberg Game Changers: Warren Buffett Revealed
https://www.youtube.com/watch?v=GJ1MW-OR-
0tI&list=PLUqYZEKhvdmUJzr4I6fDkL_WPTWL7y
U_U&in- dex=6

From: The Bill Gates Documentary FULL Edition
https://www.youtube.com/watch?v=fO2u-uxVBIc

Chapter 10: Opening Your Speech
THNKR: The Speech That Made Obama President
https:// www.youtube.com/watch?v=OFPwDe22CoY

TED: Aimee Mullins: "My twelve pairs of legs"
http://www.ted.com/talks/aimee_mullins_prosthetic_
aesthetics

TED: Simon Sinek: "How great leaders inspire action"
http://www.ted.com/talks/simon_sinek_how_great_
leaders_inspire_action

Apple Special Event: September 2014
http://www.apple.com/live/2014-sept-event/
https://www.youtube.com/watch?v=OD9ZQ9WylRM

Apple Special Event: October 22, 2013
http://www.apple.com/apple-events/october-2013/
https://www.youtube.com/watch?v=4FunXnJQxYU

Prime Minister Narendra Modi at Madison Square Garden
https://www.youtube.com/watch?v=tKx3OlHrV9I

Chapter 11: Another Copernican Revolution? (Rondo 2)

TED: Martin Seligman: "The new era of positive psychology"
http://www.ted.com/talks/martin_seligman_on_the_state_of_psychology

Shawn Achor: "The happy secret to better work"
http://www.ted.com/talks/shawn_achor_the_happy_secret_to_better_work

Chapter 12: Storytelling

TED: Andrew Stanton: "The clues to a great story"
http://www.ted.com/talks/andrew_stanton_the_clues_to_a_great_story

TEDxHogeschoolUtrecht: Steve Denning: "Leadership storytelling"
https://www.youtube.com/watch?v=RipHYzhKCuI

TEDxVancouver: Greg Power: "The Power of story"
https://www.youtube.com/watch?v=iExl_rF7zgQ TED:

Dave Lieber: "The dog of my nightmares"
https://www.youtube.com/watch?v=Xig_r8eKfeM

Kurt Vonnegut: "The shapes of stories"
https://www.youtube.com/watch?v=oP3c1h-
8v2ZQ&list=PL991B74289AE23E10

TED: Nancy Duarte: "The secret structure of great talks"
http://www.ted.com/talks/nancy_duarte_the_secret_
structure_of_great_talks

Craig Valentine's Storytelling approach
http://www.craigvalentine.com/20storiestall

Chapter 13: Orthodox PS&ST Competencies
JFK & Nixon Debates
http://www.history.com/topics/us-presidents/
kennedy-nixon-debates

Toastmasters: Your Speaking Voice
http://www.toastmasters.org/199-YourSpeakingVoice

Toastmasters: Gestures: Your Body Speaks
http://www.toastmasters.org/201-Gestures

Chapter 14: Creating the Icebreaker Speech
Barack Obama: 2004 Democratic National Convention
Keynote Address
http://www.americanrhetoric.com/speeches/
convention2004/barackobama2004dnc.htm

THNKR: The Speech That Made Obama President
https:// www.youtube.com/watch?v=OFPwDe22CoY

Chapter 15: Memorizing, Listening, and Connecting

TED: Joshua Foer: "Feats of memory that anyone can do"
http://www.ted.com/talks/joshua_foer_feats_of_
memory_anyone_can_do#t-7141

TED: Julian Treasure: "Five ways to listen better"
http://www.ted.com/talks/julian_treasure_5_ways_to_
listen_better

TED: Julian Treasure: "How to speak so that people want to listen"
http://www.ted.com/talks/julian_treasure_how_to_
speak_so_that_people_want_to_listen

TED: Julian Treasure: "Sound health in eight steps"
http://www.ted.com/talks/julian_treasure_shh_sound_
health_in_8_steps

TED: Julian Treasure: "The four ways sound affects us"
http://www.ted.com/talks/julian_treasure_the_4_ways_
sound_affects_us

TED: Julian Treasure: "Why architects need to use their ears"
http://www.ted.com/talks/julian_treasure_why_
architects_need_to_use_their_ears

Chapter 16: Finding Flow in Public Speaking and Storytelling

TED: Mihaly Csikszentmihalyi: "Flow, the secret to happiness"
http://www.ted.com/talks/mihaly_csikszentmihalyi_

on_flow

Fareed Zakaria and Steven Kotler interview
https://www. youtube.com/watch?v=Xt9xN9k3SCE

Talks at Google: Steven Kotler: The Rise of Superman:
Decoding the Science of Ultimate Human Performance
https://www.youtube.com/watch?v=y1MHyyWsMeE

HBR Steven Kotler: Create a Work Environment That
Fosters Flow
http://blogs.hbr.org/2014/05/create-a-work-
environment-that-fosters-flow/

Flow related videos
http://riseofsuperman.com/videos/

Chapter 17: Our Closing Conversation
None

About the Author

Rashid N. Kapadia, a marine engineer and project manager for decades, discovered the transformational power of public speaking, storytelling and oratory after joining a Project Management Institute (Houston) sponsored Toastmasters club.

He also discovered, to his surprise and dismay, that too many engineers and project managers seriously underappreciate—even shun—these transformative skills.

Having always seen himself as an ambassador for his storied and challenging professions, he has made it a personal mission to evangelize PS&ST to engineers and project managers around the globe.

Connect

To book the author to speak at your event or to learn more about his work and how he can help you, please visit NecessaryBridges.com or rashidkapadia.com.